The Carmelite Charism

Exploring the Biblical Roots

JAMES McCAFFREY OCD

VERITAS

First published 2004 by
Veritas Publications
7/8 Lower Abbey Street
Dublin 1
Ireland
Email publications@veritas.ie
Website www.veritas.ie

ISBN 1 85390 737 5

A catalogue record for this book is available from the British Library.

Cover design by Bill Bolger
Cover image: 'Stella Maris' Carmelite Monastery, Mount Carmel
Printed in the Republic of Ireland by Betaprint Ltd, Dublin

*Veritas books are printed on paper made from the wood pulp of
managed forests. For every tree felled, at least one tree is planted, thereby
renewing natural resources.*

*To all
who wish to pray and live the scriptures
in the spirit of Carmel*

Contents

Note on Editions Used and Symbols to Denote Them

Works by John of the Cross
The Collected Works of Saint John of the Cross, tr. Kieran Kavanaugh, OCD & Otilio Rodriguez, OCD, Washington, DC: ICS Publications, 1991, including:

A	*The Ascent of Mount Carmel*
DN	*The Dark Night*
LF	*The Living Flame of Love*
R	*Romances*
SC	*The Spiritual Canticle*

Works by Teresa of Avila
The Collected Works of St. Teresa of Avila, 3 vols, tr. Kieran Kavanaugh, OCD & Otilio Rodriguez, OCD, Washington, DC: ICS Publications, 1987, 1980 & 1985, including:

F	*The Book of Her Foundations*
IC	*The Interior Castle*
Life	*The Book of Her Life*
WP	*The Way of Perfection*

Works by Thérèse of Lisieux

LC	*St. Thérèse of Lisieux: Her Last Conversations*, tr. John Clarke, OCD, Washington, DC: ICS Publications, 1977

LT   *General Correspondence*, 2 vols, tr. John Clarke, OCD,
        Washington, DC: ICS Publications,
        1982 & 1988

PN   *The Poetry of Saint Thérèse of Lisieux*,
        tr. Donald Kinney, OCD,
        Washington, DC: ICS Publications, 1996

SS   *Story of a Soul: The Autobiography of Saint
        Thérèse of Lisieux*, tr. John Clarke, OCD,
        Washington, DC: ICS Publications, 1996

Works by Elizabeth of the Trinity

Complete Works of Elizabeth of the Trinity, 2 vols, tr. Aletheia
Kane, OCD (vol. 1) & Anne Englund Nash (vol. 2),
Washington, DC: ICS Publications, 1984 & 1995, including:

L   *Letters from Carmel*

PT   *Prayer to the Trinity*

Works by Edith Stein

HL   *The Hidden Life*, tr. Waltraut Stein,
        Washington, DC: ICS Publications,
        1992

SP   *Self-Portrait in Letters 1916-1942*,
        tr. Josephine Koeppel, OCD,
        Washington, DC: ICS Publications, 1993

Psalms

Numbering and text follow the Grail version, in *The Psalms: A
New Translation*, London & Glasgow: Fontana, 1963.

Prologue

Thomas Merton once wrote: 'There is no member of the Church who does not owe something to Carmel.' I believe we can go even further and say that Carmelite spirituality answers to the deepest need for love in every human heart. This lesson of Carmel's universal appeal I have discovered over many years. Privileged to work as director of two Carmelite retreat centres, one in Varroville, Australia, and now one in Oxford, I never cease to marvel at the hunger and thirst in people of all religions, or even none, for a deep spiritual life. This yearning, conscious or unconscious, underscores the relevance of these pages. They are all about Carmel, and Carmel is all about prayer.

Some years ago I was asked, as one of four biblical specialists, to co-author *A Biblical Prayer Journey in the Holy Land*. This book was born of a desire by the Carmelite Order to provide a specific contribution to prayer in relation both to scripture and to the lands of the bible. It afforded me a unique opportunity to share my experience of researching and teaching the scriptures and of living in the Holy Land where Carmel has its origins: in the quiet seclusion of the wadi 'Ain es Siah on the slopes of Mount Carmel. This latest book, which in many ways follows on from that earlier work, is an invitation to explore the biblical roots of Carmelite spirituality. Hence, the prominence given to the word of God in all its chapters.

In recent times, *lectio divina*, a traditional approach to personal and collective praying with the scriptures, has taken on renewed emphasis, and among the sacred writings the gospels must always take pride of place. So, Chapter 1 directs the readers wishing to pray with the evangelists 'in spirit and truth' and draws out Carmelite themes embedded deep in the gospels. Chapter 2 presents the biblical prophet Elijah, father of all Carmelites, and introduces Carmelite spirituality which has its roots and offshoots within the general framework of his life. Chapter 3 deals directly with the Carmelite *Rule* and shows how it resembles a mosaic of biblical citations or a gospel discourse rather than a legal document. Chapter 4 is devoted to St Joseph, always treasured in the 'memory' of the Church, yet a gospel figure so easily and often overlooked; the lesson of his life for every true contemplative was revived and renewed by Teresa of Avila, the great sixteenth-century reformer of Carmel. Chapter 5 portrays Mary as *the* gospel woman of prayer who has always been essential and integral to the Carmelite charism and a vital inspiration for every person of prayer. Finally, the Epilogue opens up perspectives for a sequel to *The Carmelite Charism*, on the Carmelite saints and their biblical roots.

This work is written for all who wish to deepen their relationship with God and who find that Carmelite spirituality best answers their need. It will hopefully be an encouragement for readers to steep themselves in the scriptures and to explore the vast riches of the Carmelite traditions of prayer in answer to new challenges in the Church and the world. 'Look to the future, where the Spirit is sending you,' wrote John Paul II in *Vita Consecrata*, 'in order to do even greater things' (#110). To quote Edith Stein, a Carmelite saint and now co-patroness of Europe:

The mystical stream that flows through all centuries is no spurious tributary that has strayed from the prayer life of the church – it is its deepest life. When this mystical stream breaks through traditional forms, it does so because the Spirit that blows where it will is living in it, this Spirit that has created all traditional forms and must ever create new ones.

In no small way this book is the fruit of sharing that took place in meetings of the Joint Carmelite Forum, recently formed in Ireland and Great Britain to help all branches of the Carmelite family rediscover together their shared heritage. These pages are also a tribute to the two general superiors of the Order, Joseph Chalmers OCarm and Camilo Maccise OCD, who commended the work of the Forum and encouraged greater unity throughout the entire Carmelite family. I wish to thank my OCarm and OCD brothers and sisters for their own articles and books, contributing to a better understanding of the Carmelite *Rule*, traditions and Marian devotion. Both the text and the footnotes bear ample witness to their devotional and scholarly writings. A very special word of thanks to my colleague and assistant editor of our Carmelite magazine *Mount Carmel*, Dr Joanne Mosley, for scanning these pages so carefully and professionally with her critical eye and for providing the spur I so badly needed to complete the work. Without her, it would simply never have been written.

Finally, I hope that my written word, for all its limitations, will continue to unite me with those who have listened and responded so constructively to the chapters of this book in their embryonic state. They have helped me enormously by their interest and discussions to convey the power of the word of God, speaking through the Carmelite charism, for all people and all times.

Chapter 1

Praying with the Gospels: 'In Spirit and Truth'[1]

Priority of the gospels

Some years ago, I was invited to give a retreat to the Lutheran pastors of New South Wales in Australia. Being a Carmelite, I decided to speak about prayer, and having spent most of my priestly life teaching and researching the bible, I took as my theme 'Prayer in the Gospels'.[2] At the end of the retreat, the leader thanked me and remarked, among other things, 'We actually thought that you Catholics did not know the bible.' He was voicing a common view. I like to think that Vatican II has helped to change all that and restored the scriptures to their rightful place at the centre of Catholic life: 'the force and power in the word of God is so great,' it says, 'that it remains the support and energy of the Church, the strength of faith'.[3]

Moreover, the Council also states: 'It is common knowledge that among all the Scriptures, even those of the New Testament, the Gospels have a special pre-eminence, and rightly so, for they are the principal witness of the life and teaching of the incarnate Word, our Saviour.'[4] So, perhaps even more significantly, during that retreat I was asked to share with these pastors my general approach to the gospels. Naturally, I wanted to be faithful to Catholic teaching and was totally convinced of the Church's wisdom and inspired guidance. But I did not wish to pontificate. I remember distinctly struggling with my dilemma. Then, I recalled something from my study of philosophy in the distant past. 'You cannot understand anything fully,' we were told, 'except through its causes' – through its origin or genesis; in short, how it came into being. That, in fact, is what the Church is proposing to us as the right approach to the gospels in its splendid document of Vatican II, *Dogmatic Constitution on Divine Revelation.*

A new perspective[5]

We are told to keep in mind three stages in the formation of the gospels: firstly, what Jesus did and taught in the *historical context* of his life and death; secondly, the tradition, that is, the handing on of this later in the *community of believers,* with a deeper understanding of it through the Spirit's action; and finally, the records of the evangelists themselves or the *written gospels.* These three stages are distinct but inseparably linked and entirely dependent one on the other.

If, however, we see the gospels solely as a record of the historical Jesus (first stage), we run the risk of taking the gospels as purely factual records of the words and actions of Jesus.[6] If, on the other hand, we see the gospels solely as the creation of the early community (second stage), they are without roots or foundation in the Jesus of history. The contribution here of the early community is vital, but as yet the gospels had not been written. They are not just ordinary books, like biographies or modern records of history. They are quite different. As the Council tells us: 'The sacred authors wrote the four Gospels [third stage], selecting some things from the many which had been handed on by word of mouth or in writing [second stage], reducing some of them to a synthesis, explicating some things in view of the situation of their churches, and preserving the form of proclamation but always in such fashion that they told us the honest truth about Jesus [first stage].'[7]

Prayer books of the Spirit

The Church receives the gospels from the Spirit. He is their principal author, inspiring the evangelists. The gospels were born and came into being under the Spirit's action in the heart of the praying Church and express the community's lived experience of the Christ-event. They are the Church's treasure and it is the Church that gives them to us. To approach the gospels with the Church today – open, like the first community of believers, to the action of that same Spirit – is already to pray 'in spirit and truth' (Jn 4:23.24). It is to read the word of God in the bond of love uniting all believers and to root our experience in the community dimension of the gospels. It is to pray at one with the community of all believers, guided by the Spirit who leads the Church ever deeper into eternal truth. In fact, there is no such thing as *private* prayer. Personal prayer, yes. But our prayer has value not because it is *my* prayer, but because it is the prayer of the Church. The same Spirit who prays in the Church prays in each of us: 'Likewise the Spirit helps us in our weakness; for we do not know how to pray as we ought, but the Spirit himself intercedes for us with sighs too deep for words. And he who searches all hearts knows what is the mind of the Spirit, because the Spirit intercedes for God's holy people according to the will of God' (Rm 8:26-27).

John's gospel especially – even a brief survey of it – affirms this community dimension of the Spirit's action: 'I saw the Spirit descend *like a dove* from heaven and it remained on him' (Jn 1:32). The image of the Spirit *hovering* like a bird over the primeval waters in the first lines of *Genesis* comes to mind: 'Earth was still an empty waste, and darkness hung over the deep; but already, over its waters, *stirred* the breath of God' (Gn 1:2). The evangelist is presenting Jesus as the inaugurator of a new creation. The Spirit 'abides' in Jesus who in turn is to 'baptise' or make disciples 'born of water and the Spirit' (Jn 3:5; cf. 1:33). Later in the gospel, Jesus promises the outpouring of that Spirit 'like torrents of living water' (Jn 7:38). But 'the Spirit had not yet been given because Jesus had not yet been glorified' (Jn 7:39) through his passion-resurrection. On the cross, Jesus finally 'handed over the Spirit' (Jn 19:30) to the community, and the risen Jesus 'breathed' new life into his disciples with the words: 'Receive the Holy Spirit' (Jn 20:22). The movement of the gospel comes full circle, because the promise at the outset to form disciples 'with the Holy Spirit' (Jn 1:33) is fulfilled at the end. And so, the Church is born through the Spirit and launched on its mission to the world. In union with that same Spirit, we pray the gospels within a community of faith and bear fruit in our lives through the saving power of the word.

'Our eyes fixed on Jesus'

In the Paraclete passages,[8] John specifies more precisely *how* the Spirit works as we pray the gospels.[9] The Spirit is the 'Spirit of truth' (Jn 14:17; 15:26; 16:13); Jesus *himself* is the truth (Jn 14:6). The action of the Spirit is focused on the person of Jesus and directed entirely towards him. 'Keeping our eyes fixed on Jesus', in the words of *Hebrews* (12:2), we are responding to the guidance of the Spirit in prayer. We never withdraw from the Word made flesh: 'In many and various ways God spoke of old to our fathers by the prophets; but in these last days he has spoken to us by a Son' (Hb 1:1-2). The masters of the spiritual life constantly repeat this lesson: 'In giving us his Son, his only Word (for he possesses no other),' wrote John of the Cross, 'he spoke everything to us at once in this sole Word – and he has no more to say' (2A 22:3). He is simply repeating the lesson of the gospels: 'Listen to him' (Mk 9:7).

But each evangelist in turn is a creative writer. He '*selected, synthesised* and *explicated,*' the Council tells us,[10] from the tradition(s) about Jesus with a view each to his own central insight. For Mark, Jesus is the Suffering Messiah; for Matthew, he is the obedient Israelite; for Luke, he is the Spirit-filled prophet; for John, he is the revelation in person of the Father. Each evangelist opens up new facets. Their insights are not mutually exclusive and they complement each other perfectly. The truth remains always inexhaustible; glimpses of it are always partial. It is a question of emphasis. So, each of us can pray freely with our preferred gospel passages and with our favourite evangelist. The saints did. 'The Spirit breathes where it wills' (Jn 3:8) and, led by the Spirit, each of us travels a secret path to God. It is the same Spirit who is always guiding us to the one Jesus, 'the same yesterday and today and for ever' (Hb 13:8).

An indwelling presence

There are many modes of the Spirit's presence and many variations of his action. 'I will pray the Father and he will give you another Paraclete to remain with you for ever' (Jn 14:16). Here Jesus speaks of his abiding presence in the Church through the Spirit until the end of time: 'I am with you all days' (Mt 28:20). In John Masefield's play, *The Trial of Jesus*, Procula, the wife of Pilate, asks Longinus, the centurion who stood at the foot of the cross, 'Do you think he is dead?' 'No, lady, I don't,' he replies. 'Then where is he?' she asks. And he answers, 'Let loose in the world'.[11] It is only through this Spirit that we can meet the risen Jesus present in the gospels: no longer limited, confined or conditioned by time and space.

But Jesus goes on to speak of a future presence of the Spirit after his passion-resurrection. This companion, friend, consoler, helper and advocate with the Father 'will be *in* you,' Jesus tells us (Jn 14:17), living and working deep *within* his disciples. It is an indwelling presence: 'Do you not know that you are God's temple and that God's Spirit dwells in you?... your body is a temple of the Holy Spirit within you... we are the temple of the living God' (1Cor 3:16; 6:19; 2Cor 6:16). The precise nature of the Spirit's action will only gradually unfold; it awaits further explanation. But Jesus does make clear the condition for this presence of the Spirit and his inner action: to believe and to love. We must come to the gospels with the spiritual eye of *faith*. The word of God is '*not some human thinking*', it 'is still *a living power at work* in believers' (1Th 2:13). And we must receive the Spirit with an *open heart*: 'If anyone loves me, they will keep my word, and my Father will love them, and we will come to them and make our home with them' (Jn 14:23). The message of the gospels is like 'a lamp shining in a dark place until the day [of eternity] dawns and the morning star rises in your hearts' (2Pet 1:19). We glimpse the meaning only dimly now, as in a mirror; the full riches of God's word will take an eternity to unfold.

Promptings of the Spirit
When we pray the gospels, the Spirit is our teacher: 'He will teach you everything' (Jn 14:26). Jesus explains *how*: 'He will *remind you* of all I have said to you' (Jn 14:26). This action of *recalling* has a special significance in *John*. Consider the scene where Jesus cleanses the temple and says: 'Destroy this temple, and in three days I will raise it up' (Jn 2:19). There the evangelist explains: 'When Jesus rose from the dead, his disciples *remembered* that he had said this and they believed the scripture and what he had said' (Jn 2:22). They did not merely recall the actual words of Jesus and the inspired texts of scripture. Enlightened by the Spirit, they realised afterwards how these were fulfilled in a concrete situation and saw the relevance to their own experience. So, too, when Jesus enters Jerusalem in triumph as a 'king' (Jn 12:13.15), we are told: 'At first the disciples did not understand this, but after Jesus had been glorified, they *remembered* that this had been written about him and that this had happened to him' (Jn 12:16). Again, it is not just a simple recalling of the scriptures and of an actual historical event. The past words and actions of Jesus become effective again, here and now, and take on significance and

meaning in the light of the Spirit's teaching. Jesus' words and actions become present again with their saving power. We read about them in the gospels and allow ourselves to be *read by them*. His words take on relevance and significance for us in the concrete circumstances of our own experience. The Spirit makes the word of God a word for *me* at this present moment. We should read the gospels in the light of our own *personal* experience: 'let [the] heart at length be ploughed by some keen grief or deep anxiety,' wrote Newman, 'and Scripture is *a new book*'.[12]

Jerome in his Latin version of the bible, the *Vulgate*, uses the term '*suggeret*' to translate this 'recalling' action of the Spirit (Jn 14:26). It captures the meaning beautifully. The Spirit teaches by *suggesting*. 'Do not grieve the Holy Spirit of God', we read in the *Letter to the Ephesians* (4:30), by refusing to accept his inspirations. The Spirit invites a response. There is no constraint, no force, no compulsion. He draws us gently, quietly, with his promptings in prayer: his suggestions urging us, as it were, to a free and open acceptance. The words and actions of Jesus can suddenly explode with new meaning by the power of the Spirit when something happens in our lives. This is how the Spirit works: through our life-experiences.

Thérèse of Lisieux has expressed this teaching action of the Spirit in her own original way, simply yet profoundly. She writes:

> I understand and I know from experience that: '*The kingdom of God is within you.*' Jesus has no need of books or teachers to instruct souls; He teaches without the noise of words. Never have I heard Him speak, but I feel that He is within me at each moment; He is *guiding and inspiring me* with what I must say and do. I find *just when I need them* certain lights that I had not seen until then, and it isn't most frequently during my hours of prayer

that these are most abundant but rather in the midst of my daily occupations. (SS, p.179; italics mine)

Jesus, teaching through the Spirit, answered her particular needs in the events of her life.

But no less enlightening is another passage from the writings of Thérèse. It is *her* version of the 'sacrament of the present moment':

> I have frequently noticed that Jesus doesn't want me to lay up *provisions*; He nourishes me *at each moment* with a totally new food; I find it within me without my knowing how it is there. I believe it is Jesus Himself hidden in the depths of my poor little heart: He is giving me the grace of acting within me, making me think of all He desires me to do *at the present moment.* (SS, p.165; italics mine)

Prayer of the heart

Pascal once wrote that 'the heart has its reasons'.[13] The psalms also speak of 'the thoughts of [the] heart' (cf. Ps 18:15). For the author of *Hebrews*, the word of God is 'sharper than any two-edged sword, piercing to the division of soul and spirit, of joints and marrow, and discerning the thoughts and intentions of the heart' (4:12). The Latin rendering for the act of 'recalling' is *recordare* – from *re*-again, *cor*-heart, *dare*-to give – meaning precisely: giving (handing over or entrusting) something to the heart. This is the movement of God's word from the head to the heart, as it seeps into the deepest core of our being under the 'recalling' action of the Spirit. Isaiah compares God's word to 'the rain and the snow' descending into the soil, 'making it yield and giving growth' (55:10). When we read the gospels, the word of God is destined ultimately to penetrate our hearts, the place where we commune directly with God in prayer.

The new *Catechism of the Catholic Church* explains the biblical sense of heart:

The heart is the dwelling-place where I am, where I live; according to the Semitic or biblical expression, the heart is the place 'to which I withdraw'. The heart is our hidden centre, beyond the grasp of our reason and of others; only the Spirit of God can fathom the human heart and know it fully. The heart is the place of decision, deeper than our psychic drives. It is the place of truth, where we choose life or death. It is the place of encounter, because as image of God we live in relation: it is the place of covenant. (#2563)

The scriptures speak of the heart more than a thousand times and call it the perennial spring of prayer. Jesus complains in the words of Isaiah: 'This people honours me with their lips, but their heart is far from me' (Mk 7:6; cf. Is 29:13). Prayer is indeed an affair of the heart, where the word of God sinks deep within us and is 'alive and active' through the presence of the Spirit. This is the *new heart* promised by the prophets: 'I will put my law within them, and I will write it upon their hearts... A new heart I will give you and a new spirit I will put within you' (Jer 31:33; Ez 36:26). This place 'within' – that is, the heart – is, for the followers of Jesus, the 'inner room' where he invites his disciples to pray: 'When you pray, go into your inner room and shut the door and pray to your Father who is in secret; and your Father who sees in secret will reward you' (Mt 6:6).

The prayer of the heart feeds on the word of God. Vatican II reminds all believers that 'prayer should accompany the reading of sacred Scripture, so that God and man may talk together; for "we speak to Him when we pray; we hear Him when we read the divine sayings."'[14] It also states that 'the word of God... remains... the food of the soul, the pure and perennial source of spiritual life'; and 'in the sacred books, the Father who is in heaven meets His children with great love and speaks with them'.[15]

'Into all truth'

As we pray the gospels, John tells us, 'the Spirit will lead [us] into all truth' (Jn 16:13). This means, literally, 'will guide [us] along the *way* of truth'. The phrase echoes the previous words of Jesus: 'I am the *way*, the truth and the life' (Jn 14:6). Both terms – 'way' and 'lead' – recall the *way* God *led* his people on their exodus journey. In the life of Jesus, this desert journey becomes a *new exodus*. It is his passage out of this world to the Father: literally, his '*passover*' from death to life (Jn 13:1). This, too, is the pattern of the Spirit's action when we pray the gospels. At one with Jesus, we are led by him along the way of the exodus through the paschal mystery, dying and rising as we journey in faith 'into all truth' revealed in the Jesus of the gospels. Faith is not something fixed or static. It is powerful, dynamic – a movement. Significantly, John never uses the noun 'faith'. It is always the verb 'believe'. Nor does he ever speak of believing 'in'; it is always believing 'into' Jesus. Elizabeth of the Trinity captures beautifully this movement of living faith. She prays: 'may each minute carry me further into the depths of Your Mystery… May I never leave You there alone but be wholly present, my faith wholly vigilant, wholly adoring, and wholly surrendered to Your creative Action' (PT).[16]

The truth of God's word can always unfold more fully as we pray the gospels. St Ephraem, one of the Eastern Fathers, expressed the idea well:

> Lord, who can grasp all the wealth of just one of your words? What we understand is much less than what we leave behind, like thirsty people who drink from a fountain. For your word, Lord, has many shades of meaning just as those who study it have many different

points of view. The Lord has coloured his words with many hues so that each person who studies it can see in it what he loves. He has hidden many treasures in his word so that each of us is enriched as we meditate on it. The word of God… is like that rock opened in the *desert* that from all its parts gave forth a spiritual drink.[17]

When God is silent

God spoke to his people in this way: 'I will lure her into the *desert* and there I will speak to her heart' (Hos 2:14). But what about the times when nothing happens or *seems* to happen when we pray with the gospels: when there are only distractions, confusion, emptiness and dryness of spirit? There is no voice; no one answers; no one seems to hear. Then we are sharing the desert experience of the people of God. Again, Thérèse explains how even the scriptures seem at times to fall silent:

> Frequently, we descend into the fertile valleys where our heart loves to nourish itself, *the vast field of the scriptures* which has so many times opened before us to pour out its rich treasures in our favour; this vast field seems to us to be a *desert, arid and without water*… We know no longer where we are; instead of peace and light, we find only *turmoil* or at least *darkness*… We are still not as yet in our homeland, and *trial must purify us as gold in the crucible. At times, we believe ourselves abandoned.* Alas!… the vain noises that disturb us, are they within us or outside us? We do not know… but Jesus really knows. He sees our sadness *and suddenly His gentle voice makes itself heard*, a voice more gentle than the springtime breeze (LT 165; italics mine)

Patience, perseverance and determination are needed while the seed of God's word is edging its way silently towards the light through the darkness of the earth: 'Night and day, while [the sower] sleeps, when he is awake, the seed is sprouting and growing; how, he does not know. Of its own accord the land produces first the shoot, then the ear, then the full grain in the ear' (Mk 4:27-28). If we are lost 'in the valley of darkness' (Ps 22:4), it is only for a while.

A refiner's fire

But what is happening in the darkness? The Spirit is drilling the roots of self-love, healing and purifying the heart. 'The heart is more devious than any other thing,' Jeremiah says, 'perverse too: who can pierce its secrets? I the Lord search to the heart, I probe the loins' (17:9-10). At the same time, the Spirit is forming us in the likeness of Jesus. There is something remarkable about the way the prophet Malachi describes God's purifying and transforming action: 'He shall sit as a refiner and purifier of silver' (3:3). A silversmith was once invited to explain. 'But do you sit watching while the work of refining is going on?' 'Oh, yes,' he replied, 'I must sit with my eyes constantly fixed on the furnace, for if the necessary time be extended in the slightest degree, the silver will be tarnished.' The gospels have eyes. The Lord's searching gaze is always fixed on us in times of trial and darkness as we wrestle with the word of God. But the silversmith added this further and most striking observation: 'I only know that the process of refining is complete,' he said, 'when I see my own image reflected in the silver.' The lesson is telling: when God sees his image reflected in us, then his work is complete.

This effect of God's purifying flame is described in many different ways. It is like a journey out of darkness into the light: 'He who follows me walks not in darkness but will have the light of life' (Jn 8:12; cf. 9:5; 12:35). It is equivalently a call to repentance: 'Repent, for the kingdom of heaven is at hand' (Mt 4:17; cf. Lk 24:47) – repentance in the gospel sense of the word, meaning a change of mind and heart. As the scriptures tell us, it is a call to put on the mind of Christ: 'Let this mind be in you that was also in Christ Jesus' (Ph 2:5), Paul says – an invitation that takes many different forms: 'renewal in the spirit of your minds' (Eph 4:23), 'transformation by the renewal of your mind' (Rm 12:2), a 'new birth' through the Spirit (Jn 3:3.5), 'a new creation in Christ' (2Cor 5:17), putting on a 'new nature' (Col 3:10), 'a sharing in the divine nature' (2Pet 1:4). It is this creative action of God through the Spirit that seals our hearts with the features of Jesus: we are 'created after the likeness of God' (Eph 4:24) and 'conformed to the image of his Son' (Rm 8:29). Paul sums this up beautifully: 'We all, with unveiled faces, reflecting as in a mirror the glory of the Lord, are being changed into his likeness from one degree of glory to another. This is the working of the Lord who is the Spirit' (2Cor 3:18).

A listening heart

To hear the voiceless word of God in the gospels, we need a listening ear. It is rare to find someone who really listens. I once met such a person! It was Mother Teresa of Calcutta. When I met her she was washing the face of a leper. Her eyes were fixed on him, his on her. No word passed between them. But this was an alert stillness, an eloquent sharing. Here was someone who was really listening – quiet, fully alive, focused, attentive. Hers was a *listening heart*. Her whole bearing was a lesson in total presence. The Christian Brother who introduced me to her told her that I was teaching scripture in the seminary of Alwaye in Kerala, South India. She glanced at me for a moment with her piercing eyes, then turned back to attend to the leper and said, 'We need the word of God for this.' I had loved scripture, studied it, taught it, written about it. But here was a woman of deep and simple faith. *She* really listened to it, lived it and put it into practice. It had borne fruit in her life, not just thirty or sixty but a hundredfold. The record of her service to the poor and the rejects of society, the marginalised and the deprived, is there to prove it. My approach to the gospels has never been the same since I met her.

This is a listening much deeper than just hearing words. Only a highly sensitive heart can catch the deeper resonance in another's voice, beat in unison with it and often feel the secret pain. This is empathy. It is the listening of a true disciple: 'Morning by morning [God] makes my ear alert to listen like a disciple' (Is 50:4). To listen keenly in this way carries us deep into stillness and silence. An Australian poet, Judith Wright, expresses this well:

> Silence is the rock where I shall stand.
> Oh, when I strike it with my hand
> may the artesian waters spring
> from that dark source I long to find.[18]

A listening God

Listening opens up to us the inner mystery of God. Jesus is the listening heart of God made flesh, always alert and attentive to the word of his Father: 'I have made known to you all that I have *heard* from my Father' (Jn 15:15). His early years were passed in listening: 'He went down to Nazareth and was obedient to them' (Lk 2:51) – 'obedient' in the root sense of the word, which means literally 'to listen' (from the Latin *ob-audire*). We find him in the temple, listening to the teachers and asking them questions. His were the probings of a listener waiting expectantly for an answer.

The Spirit also listens. 'He will not speak from himself,' Jesus tells us, 'but whatever he *hears* he will speak' (Jn 16:13). When we read the gospels at one with this listening Spirit, we are drawn into God through Jesus who is always turned '*towards* the bosom of the Father' (Jn 1:18). Jesus is not just *in* the Father, but the whole thrust of his being is a dynamic movement directed eternally *into* the heart of God (Jn 1:1). He is always open to receive everything from the Father and returns everything to him in total self-giving, just as he passes on everything in turn to others: 'All that the Father has is mine; therefore I said that [the Spirit] will take what is mine and declare it to you' (Jn 16:15). To share this eternal listening in the heart of God is to enter a loving communion of persons – Father, Son and Spirit – a silent dialogue, a timeless giving and receiving, an eternal exchange of love. It is to pray.

Teresa of Avila speaks of prayer as an exchange or dialogue of love with 'Him who we know loves us' (*Life* 8:5). Prayer is not about *thinking* much, she tells us. That's meditation – a preamble to prayer. Prayer is essentially about *loving* – a fling of our heart to the heart of God or, for John of the Cross, 'a secret and peaceful and loving inflow of God, which, if not hampered, fires the soul in the spirit of love' (1DN 10:6). Thérèse of Lisieux sums up this teaching well: 'you know,' she says, 'that I myself do not see the Sacred Heart as everybody else. I think that the Heart of my Spouse is mine alone, just as mine is His alone, and I speak to Him then in the solitude of this delightful heart to heart, while waiting to contemplate Him one day face to face' (LT 122). Or, to quote the words of the Irish poet, Patrick Kavanagh, who speaks of the power of love unleashed through prayer:

> One love lone flame
> > In a dark cell
> Makes fuel of firmaments
> > And dims out Hell.[19]

'Come and see'

To encounter Jesus in reading the gospels is an invitation to be challenged and to challenge others in turn. The story of the Samaritan woman illustrates the point. She first meets Jesus herself and then invites others to share her experience: 'Come, see a man who told me all that I ever did' (Jn 4:29; cf. 4:39). She does not force others; she invites an answer: 'Can this be the Christ?' (Jn 4:29). The Samaritans accept her witness. They come to Jesus and discover him for themselves. The story reaches a climax when the Samaritans profess their own faith in Jesus: 'They said to the woman, "It is no longer because of your words that we believe, for we have heard for ourselves, and we know that this is indeed the Saviour of the world"' (Jn 4:42).

We find the same pattern of witness in John's account of the call of the first disciples (1:35-51). Jesus also invites them to 'come and see' (1:39; cf. 1:46). It is his challenge to a personal faith-encounter with himself. Each of his followers in turn goes off to share his own experience with others and invites them to a personal encounter with Jesus. We find a series of revealing titles for Jesus as the truth about him dawns gradually on the disciples: 'Rabbi', 'Messiah', 'Son of God', 'King of Israel' (Jn 1:38.41.49). Their meeting with him becomes a progressive exploration of his mystery. But self-discovery, too, is the effect of their encounter (1:42.47), just as it was for the Samaritan woman. Self-knowledge in the light of Jesus is the fruit of a prayerful reading of the gospels.

Witness of an Easter people

Jesus says that the Spirit 'will reveal to you the things that are to come' (Jn 16:13). This is not a promise to foretell the future. John is referring here to the imminent events of the passion-resurrection of Jesus about to take place: the 'hour' of John's gospel where passion and resurrection are inseparably linked, two complementary aspects of the one paschal mystery. The Spirit will *reveal* this 'hour' – not just throwing light on it, manifesting it to the disciples, but also making it present in the Church until the end of time. It is like a still-point in the vortex of salvation history: everything pivots around it – past, present and future. The gospels were written in the light of it and that is how we should read them. They are documents composed with hindsight, after the passion-resurrection, by witnesses of the resurrection.[20] In the same way we, too, must proclaim the gospel message: as witnesses to the risen Jesus. We are an Easter people, a people redeemed. In his record of a celebrated court case, Whittaker Chambers explains this kind of witness:

> I was a witness... A man is not primarily a witness *against* something. That is only incidental to the fact that he is a witness *for* something. A witness, in the sense that I am using the word, is a man whose life and faith are so completely one that when the challenge comes to step out and testify for his faith, he does so, disregarding all risks, accepting all consequences.[21]

An enlightened heart

The Spirit working in us as witness 'will *convince the world* of sin and of righteousness and of judgment' (Jn 16:8). In fact, this translation of the *RSV* is misleading. So, too, is the rendering of the *Jerusalem Bible*: 'he will *show the world* how wrong it was...'. What the original text means is that the Spirit will show *us* (not the *world*) how wrong the world is with regard to sin, righteousness and judgment (cf. Jn 3:19-21). The 'world' here is the world of darkness, the world that 'cannot receive' the Spirit (Jn 14:17). The Spirit will reveal everything to believers, showing sin, righteousness and judgment in clarity for what they really are.

The Spirit will expose the true nature of '*sin*' as disbelief because, in the words of Jesus, 'they do not believe in me' (Jn 16:9). This is emphatic: they refuse to believe in him – a free, deliberate choice. He will also show '*righteousness*' clearly for what it is: who is in the right – Jesus, not the world! Again, Jesus explains: 'because I go to the Father', referring to his victorious return through his passion-resurrection; and 'you will see me no more' (Jn 16:10), meaning that he will be invisible to the naked eye, and visible only to the eyes of faith. The Spirit will also bring to light the true meaning of '*judgment*'. Jesus clarifies: 'This is the judgment, that the light has come into the world, and people preferred darkness to the light' (Jn 3:19). In choosing darkness, they cut themselves off from Jesus and condemn themselves. Jesus came for 'judgment' or, literally, *decision* (Jn 9:39: *krima*) – with a challenge freely to accept or reject his word. Like the Spirit, we too must bear witness to the gospel values – values that we have assimilated in prayer. Others are free to accept or reject them. To reject them is to condemn one's self; to accept them is to be drawn by Jesus 'out of darkness into his own wonderful light' (1Pet 2:9).

Power in weakness

Jesus challenges his disciples to bear witness, warning them of future trials, difficulties and persecutions: 'I have said these things to keep you from being scandalised' (Jn 16:1) – in the gospel sense of 'falling away' or 'losing faith' in Jesus (cf. Mk 6:3; Jn 6:61). In this perspective, the paschal mystery always present in the Church takes on heightened significance: 'A servant is not greater than his master. If they persecuted me they will persecute you... They hated me without a cause' (Jn 15:20.25). Hardships, rejection by others and persecution for the sake of the gospel plunge us ever deeper into the paschal mystery. They are a spur to return again and again to pray the gospels in the light of the passion-resurrection: 'We were so utterly, unbearably crushed that we despaired of life itself,' Paul writes. 'Why, we felt that we had received *the sentence of death*; but that was to make us rely not on ourselves but on *God who raises the dead*... on him we have set our hope' (2Cor 1:8-10). Again, Whittaker Chambers describes this kind of witness:

I do not know any way to explain why God's grace touches a man who seems unworthy of it. But neither do I know any other way to explain how a man like myself – tarnished by life, unprepossessing, not brave – could prevail so far against the powers of the world arrayed almost solidly against him, to destroy him and defeat his truth. In this sense, I am [a]…witness to God's grace and to the fortifying power of faith.[22]

So, too, Mary was a witness to God's grace at work in her and to 'the fortifying power of faith'. To make her mind and heart our own is to read the gospels in a fresh and entirely new way.

Lectio divina

The insights which we have discovered about praying with the gospels 'in spirit and truth' may be beautiful and sublime, but they can so easily remain at the level of theory. They need to be translated into an *actual* experience of praying with scripture. As with all quiet prayer, it is important for us to find a place where we can be silent, undisturbed. We still the mind and calm the senses as best we can, for example by breathing slowly, deeply and rhythmically. This can be helpful as a prelude to reading the word.[23] There are many ways of doing *lectio divina* and methods abound.[24] But to read the word in the spirit of Carmel is to pray it with the heart of Mary: to put on the dispositions of her inner life. She is a living witness to the quiet working of God's grace within her as she responds in concrete circumstances to the challenge of God's word. A glance at her life provides us with some practical helps that we all need, as individuals or as groups, for a simple and renewed approach to the traditional *lectio divina* in a way that is accessible to all.

There are *no barriers* when Mary listens to the word. There must be none for us either. She is at ease, *relaxed with God* – aware that she is the object of his special love. This *awareness of his love for us* must also be our entry point into prayer: we, too, are his 'most highly favoured ones'. We must *stand before God just as we are*: 'Behold the handmaid of the Lord' (Lk 1:38), and he looks on his servant 'in her lowliness': we come as weak, frail, *vulnerable and contrite sinners*, unmasked before a God whose 'mercy is from age to age'. Mary comes before him knowing that he who is mighty has done – and can still do – great things for her. We must start with that same *attitude of trust* and be ready to *risk everything* on the truth of his word. Let us *listen* to the word, *be challenged*, and *surrender ourselves* to it. If we wish, we can say all this in an eloquently simple gesture with empty and upturned hands, *waiting to receive* whatever God wants to say to us and ask of us.

Mary's faith unlocks the real secret of her approach to the word: 'Blessed is she who believed that the word spoken to her by the Lord would be fulfilled' (Lk 1:45). We, too, must come to the bible in a *spirit of faith* – a faith like hers ever searching for a deeper meaning and understanding of what is happening, here and now, in our lives. So, we begin with an *act of faith*, opening our inner eye to the action of the Spirit who will 'come upon' us as he did for Mary. We *invoke the Holy Spirit*. For this, we may choose a prayer of our own liking. Perhaps it will be a traditional one such as: 'Come, Holy Spirit'. Or, if we prefer, we can formulate a prayer in our own words. Reading the gospels, open with Mary to the action of the Spirit, will centre us directly on her Son. We must always bear in mind that the inspired texts, both the old and the new, speak of him. So, we *focus on Jesus*, together with Mary who was the first to fix her eyes on the Word made flesh: 'The Mother gazed in sheer wonder,' wrote John of the Cross (R 9). To contemplate with the eyes of Mary is to see Jesus.

We now *read the word*. We select *a short passage* and *repeat it slowly, more than once* – *reflecting* on it and *listening* to it deep within. We *wait* for a word or phrase to stand out from the

page. Like Mary we *meditate* on these words, 'pondering' them
and 'treasuring them in our heart'. The word of God must
descend from head to heart. This is often a painful journey into
the very core of our being. We read the word with our life's
experience and *let our life's experience be read* by it in turn.
Gradually, we ourselves become a living word: this has nothing
to do with sublime heights beyond our reach – it is the effect of
direct contact with the power of God's saving love released
through the word by the Spirit. It is only love that can change
and transform us. The word touches our heart and *we let our
hearts go out in love.*

We now begin to *pray the word.* We lay bare before the Lord
whatever surfaces for us from the word: aspirations and
longings, disappointments and hopes, concern and gratitude,
joys and sorrows – all rising from the wellsprings of the heart.
We voice to him in silence all our inmost thoughts and desires.
Sharing with God our needs, and the needs of others, we can
follow the Virgin at Cana who merely stated the situation, then
trusted God to provide the answer: 'They have no wine' (Jn
2:3). Nor must we be shy about exposing to him our worries,
questions, even our doubts. Like Mary, we will surely feel at
times bewildered and confused: 'How can this come about?…
[She] did not understand the saying' (Lk 1:34; 2:50). We may
be wrestling with an urgent problem, seeking an answer that
never seems to come: 'Why have you done this to us? Your
father and I have been searching for you anxiously' (Lk 2:48).
As we walk in the light of the word, we will find a new self-
knowledge, content like Mary in our 'lowliness' as we discover
a God of mercy who exalts the humble. Like her, too, we may
find ourselves brimming with thanksgiving and praise: 'The
Almighty has done great things for me, holy is his name' (Lk
1:49). Or we might just give ourselves over to an inner current
of joy: 'My spirit rejoices in God, my Saviour' (Lk 1:47). As our
quiet prayer continues, it may give way to an ever deeper

stillness. We will now find ourselves drawn into silent *contemplation* with a simple glance of love towards Jesus. In spirit we stand with Mary, gazing on her Son – just as she stood at the foot of the cross, communing with Jesus in love and accepting from him there her future mission.

To *accept the word* is to respond to God's invitation by saying, 'Let it be done to me according to your word' (1:38). Mary's reply must always be our own, even when the page before us does not immediately 'speak' to us. It may be that the seed of the word is still sinking into the soil of our hearts. It will thrust up shoots at its proper time. This may be a slow, gradual, imperceptible process. The spiritual life is, in any case, a marathon, not a sprint: we must *walk at God's pace*, as Mary did when puzzling over the angel's enigmatic message and awaiting its unfolding in God's own time. We must not anticipate God's action but remain *always open* to its fulfilment, even when God seems to be silent, no longer 'speaking' his word. We need *constancy, determination* and *resolve* in this desert experience, trusting in the goodness of God and the wisdom of his word – holding firm, as Mary did, when her initial *fiat* was finally tested on Calvary.

The fruits – our *action*, in answer to God's word – will take many forms. But Mary's experience shows that they will be essentially the same: *compassion*, hurrying to our neighbour in need, just as Mary 'arose and went with haste into the hill country of Judah' (Lk 1:39) to tend to her cousin Elizabeth; *witness*, inviting others to come and listen to Jesus: 'Do whatever he tells you' (Jn 2:5), and announcing to the world the wonders of God's goodness: 'My soul proclaims the greatness of the Lord' (Lk 1:46); *solidarity with the community of believers* as we pray, for them and with them, together with the mother of God and mother of the church who was 'joined in continuous prayer' with the first disciples (Acts 1:14). We wait, like them, for the outpouring of the Holy Spirit who will bring back to our memory the word we have read, spoken by Mary's Son.

25

Ultimately, to listen to the word is to be conformed to Jesus who 'went down to Nazareth and was obedient' (Lk 2:51) – 'obedient' in the radical sense of that word as 'listening'. Mary listened to Jesus and he listened to her. That is what reading the gospels 'in spirit and truth' should mean for us all: a perfect dialogue of love.

Notes

1   An earlier version of this chapter was delivered as a talk at the Annual Conference of Our Lady's Catechists at Plater College, Oxford, on April 25th, 2003.

2   See also the author's *Prayer – The Heart of the Gospels*, Oxford: Teresian Press, 1985; *Thirsting For God in Scripture*, Locust Valley, NY: Living Flame Press, 1984; *A Biblical Prayer Journey in the Holy Land* [co-authored], Burgos: Editorial Monte Carmelo, 1998.

3   *Dei Verbum* (*Dogmatic Constitution on Divine Revelation*) 21.

4   *Ibid.* 18.

5   For a fuller discussion of this new perspective on the gospels in *Dei Verbum* (*Dogmatic Constitution on Divine Revelation*), see ch. 3, section 'The three-layered approach'.

6   Note that to see the gospels as *purely* factual records – like a verbatim account or a series of snapshots – is only one dimension of the historical approach. There are two other possible approaches closely allied to this. One is to see the records as *completely* factual: this is not the case and would imply a view that only verbatim accounts contain the whole truth, whereas in fact the gospels are true at a much deeper level, whether or not the reported words and actions of Jesus are the actual ones spoken and done by the historical Jesus. The other, more pernicious, approach is fundamentalism: not only taking the words of Jesus as an accurate record, but also applying them literally to current situations where they are then twisted out of context, such as refusing to call one's father 'Father' (cf. Mt 23:9) or trying to remove mountains by faith (cf. Mt 17:20). For a Catholic response to fundamentalism, see Raymond E. Brown, SS, *Reading the Gospels with the Church: From Christmas through Easter*, Cincinnati, OH: St Anthony Messenger Press, 1996, pp. 77-86.

7   *Dei Verbum* (*Dogmatic Constitution on Divine Revelation*) 19.

8   Jn 14:16-17.26; 15:26-27; 16:7-11.12-15.

9   See Ignace de La Potterie, SJ & Stanislaus Lyonnet, SJ, *The Christian Lives by the Spirit*, New York: Alba House, 1971, ch. 3, 'The Paraclete', pp. 57-77.

10 *Dei Verbum* (*Dogmatic Constitution on Divine Revelation*) 19.

11 John Masefield, *The Trial of Jesus*, London: William Heinemann, 1925, pp. 95-6.

12 John Henry Newman, *An Essay in Aid of a Grammar of Assent*, Garden City, New York: Image Books, 1955, p. 80; italics mine.

13 From his *Pensées*, IV, 277 (Brunschvicg numbering).

14 *Dei Verbum* (*Dogmatic Constitution on Divine Revelation*) 25.

15 *Ibid.* 21.

16 For an alternative translation, see the author's 'Prayer of Bl. Elizabeth of the Trinity – A New Translation', *Mount Carmel*, vol. 47/3, 1999, p. 51.

17 From St Ephraem, *Commentary on the Diatessaron*, quoted in *Divine Office*, vol. I, p. 518; italics mine.

18 Judith Wright, *Collected Poems 1942-1970*, Sydney: Angus & Robertson, 1975, p. 123.

19 From 'Lone Flame', in Patrick Kavanagh, *The Complete Poems*, New York: The Peter Kavanagh Hand Press / Newbridge: The Goldsmith Press, 1972, p. 12.

20 Acts 1:21-22; 2:32; 3:15; cf. 1Cor 15:14; Rm 10:9.

21 From Whittaker Chambers, *Witness*, New York: Random House, 1952, p. 5.

22 *Ibid.*, p. 6.

23 For relaxation techniques in the context of prayer, see: Laurence Freeman, OSB, *Christian Meditation: Your Daily Practice*, Rydalmere, NSW: Hunt & Thorpe, 1994; James Borst, MHM, *A Method of Contemplative Prayer*, Homebush, NSW: Society of St Paul, 1979; J. de Rooy, SJ, *Tools for Meditation*, Pinner: The Grail, 1976; Anthony de Mello, SJ, *Sadhana – A Way to God: Christian Exercises in Eastern Form*, Garden City, New York: Image Books, 1984.

24 See especially the following publications: Brigeen Wilson, OCD: 'A Living Power Among Us: A New Springtime of the Gospel', *Mount Carmel*, vol. 49/2, 2001, pp. 8-17; *ibid.*, 'A Living Power Among Us: Called Together by the Word', *Mount Carmel*, vol. 50/1, 2002, pp. 27-35; Carlos Mesters, OCarm, *Lectio Divina*, Melbourne:

Carmelite Communications, 1999; Michel de Verteuil, CSSp, *Eucharist as Word: Lectio Divina and the Eucharist,* Dublin: Veritas, 2001; Mariano Magrassi, OSB, *Praying the Bible: An Introduction to Lectio Divina,* Collegeville, MN: Liturgical Press, 1998. Ernest E. Larkin, OCarm provides a helpful discussion of *lectio divina* in relation to two popular forms of contemplative prayer: see his 'The Carmelite Tradition and Centering Prayer/Christian Meditation', in Keith J. Egan, T. OCarm (ed.), *Carmelite Prayer: A Tradition for the 21st Century,* New York & Mahwah, NJ: Paulist Press, 2003, pp. 202-22 (see especially pp. 205-8).

Chapter 2

The Heritage of Elijah: Introducing Carmelite Spirituality[1]

Origins

The Carmelite Order was born in the Holy Land.[2] At the end of the twelfth century a small group of hermits – some of them crusaders – had settled on the slopes of Mount Carmel, the mountain range from which the Order derives its name. These were the first Carmelites. The evidence of their original settlement still survives in the well-preserved ruins of both monastery and chapel beside the 'Spring of Elijah' in the wadi 'Ain es Siah. In these idyllic surroundings, the Carmelites lived their daily round of prayer and work as hermits in community, with a limited apostolic outreach.[3]

Early in the thirteenth century (1206-14), they asked Albert, Patriarch of Jerusalem for a rule of life in conformity with their proposed lifestyle (*propositum*). He responded with what is now called the *Primitive Rule of Carmel*. It is a brief document, the briefest of all the rules of that time, and extremely flexible. It is not a rigid set of laws and regulations. It resembles a mosaic of scriptural quotations, more like a biblical discourse of Matthew's gospel than a legal document. Like the bible itself, it has an inner dynamism capable of growing, expanding and developing under the breath of the Spirit in response to the changing circumstances of the time.[4]

Expelled later by the Saracens (1238 onwards), the Carmelites were uprooted from the Holy Land and emigrated to Europe. There they took on a wider ministry (preaching, teaching, administering the sacraments) and were accepted as one of the new mendicant orders, so-called from the verb *mendicare*, 'to beg'. Such, among others, were the Franciscans and Dominicans. The lifestyle of the first Carmelites grew and developed in creative fidelity to the original inspiration of Albert's *Rule* during the first forty years of their existence. So, a final text, emended and adapted to the changing conditions of time and space, was finally approved in 1247.[5]

Father of all Carmelites

Unlike other religious families, the Carmelites have no founder or foundress as such. For the Teresian branch, Teresa of Avila and John of the Cross are popularly regarded as the sixteenth-century founders. In fact, they were *reformers*. When asked about their roots – identity, spirituality and credentials – the early Carmelites could not call on a Benedict or a Francis of Assisi. They simply turned to Elijah whose exploits still clung like sacred memories to the mountain of Carmel's origin. It is to this fiery prophet of Mount Carmel that they looked for inspiration and the embodiment of their vision and ideals.[6] 'Elijah arose like a fire,' we are told, 'his word burning like a torch' (Sir 48:1). These words are emblazoned beneath a statue of the great prophet himself at 'The Place of Sacrifice' (Muhraqa) on the eastern slopes of Mount Carmel in the Holy Land. His powerful figure stands with flaming sword raised aloft, a false prophet slain at his feet, and his eyes reaching out across an endless plain, as if to proclaim a message relevant for all people and all time.

Elijah appears on the stage of history like a thunderbolt, to announce a drought with these stark credentials: 'As the Lord God of Israel lives, in whose presence I stand' (1Kgs 17:1). The prophet is father of all Carmelites – his words, 'with zeal have I been zealous for the Lord God of hosts' (1Kgs 19:10.14), adorning our crest. He is a vigorous personality and one of contrasts, appearing suddenly – only to disappear again just as suddenly into solitude: a man of action and a man of prayer. Carmelites find in him an exemplar of their spirit and mission for today's world.[7] We can easily discover the roots and offshoots of Carmelite spirituality within the general framework and unfolding events of his life.[8]

God alone

The Carmelite way is a journey of the heart. It is like the exodus experience of God's people and their meeting with Yahweh in the wilderness as described in *Deuteronomy*: 'Remember how Yahweh your God led you for forty years in the wilderness, to humble you and to test you in order to know your inmost heart' (Dt 8:2). This exodus theme runs all through the poetry and commentaries of John of the Cross: 'One dark night, / fired with love's urgent longings… / I *went out* unseen, / my house being now all stilled' (DN, stanza 1; italics mine). And again: 'I *went out* calling you, but you were gone' (SC, stanza 1; italics mine). On their desert march, the Israelites encounter a transcendent God who challenges them with the radical demands of his covenant: 'I am the Lord your God, who brought you out of the land of Egypt… You shall have no other gods before me' (Ex 20:2-3).

Salvation history repeats itself in the story of Elijah. The prophet confronts the people again with these same radical demands. They are wavering, dithering, 'hobbling now on one foot, now on another' (1Kgs 18:21), vacillating and yielding to the lure of false gods. He challenges them to conversion: 'If the Lord is God, follow him; but if Baal, follow him' (1Kgs 18:21). Their choice is clear and uncompromising: 'The Lord, he is God; the Lord, he is God' (1Kgs 18:39).

In this sense, too, Carmelite asceticism is radical, but it is never rigid, stark or insensitive. It is like falling in love: meeting someone special who captivates and kindles a passion deeper than other, lesser loves. Then, all these other affections gradually fall into place. It is like discovering the gospel 'pearl of great price', the 'treasure hidden in a field'. It is a question of priorities: 'You shall love the Lord your God with all your heart, with all your soul and with all your might' (Dt 6:5). It costs all, as Paul explains: 'What we have to do is to give up everything that does not lead to God' (Tit 2:12).

The Carmelite is called to search in every dark and hidden crevice of the human heart for those lurking demons of Israel's desert experience, the 'venomous serpents and scorpions' as they are called, inhabiting the wilderness (Dt 8:15). We find this same imagery again in Teresa of Avila, when she compares the human heart to an 'interior castle' surrounded by 'snakes and vipers and poisonous creatures' (IC I:2:14). They represent the snares of worldly attachments, our false gods, which have become non-negotiables in our lives. We must not replace God with our idols – that is, our disordered or inordinate desires. The Carmelite way is a journey *into* God with the freedom of an undivided heart. Only God suffices. He alone can satisfy our deepest hunger.

Not changing *God*, changing *us*

Carmelite spirituality is essentially about prayer. So, Elijah holds a special place for us as the great contemplative. The prophet himself describes his own personal relationship with Yahweh: 'As the Lord God of Israel lives, in whose presence I stand' (1Kgs 17:1; cf. 18:15). He is always the one who *stands before the face of the living God*; his prayer is always looking into the face of God. This is to pray like Jesus in the gospels – standing, always and everywhere, before the face of his Father. This, too, is Carmelite prayer: resting with God in an eye-to-eye communion of love. Elizabeth of the Trinity writes (quoting her spiritual director, Fr Vallée): 'The contemplative is a being who lives in the radiance of the Face of Christ, who enters into the mystery of God, not in the light that flows from human thought, but in that created by the word of the Incarnate Word' (L 158).

The spirit of Elijah is first refined and tempered in solitude at the brook Cherith.[9] Meanwhile, the people are disposed for God's intervention by three years of parched waiting. A dramatic contest ensues. Elijah addresses the God of the covenant – the One who is always pursuing his people in search of their love: 'so that this people may know that you, Yahweh, are God and are winning back their hearts' (1Kgs 18:37). Here Elijah is praying in response to a God of love, 'a God merciful and gracious, slow to anger, and abounding in steadfast love and faithfulness, keeping steadfast love for thousands, forgiving iniquity and transgression and sin' (Ex 34:6-7). Carmelite prayer, too, is a response to love. For Teresa, it is an intimate sharing among friends, a communing with the God 'who we know loves us' (*Life* 8:5). It is not about thinking much; it is about loving much (cf. F 5:2).

Elijah's prayer stands out in striking contrast to that of the false prophets of Baal. Their antics are a parody on true prayer. Howling and shrieking, they limp around the altar hurling empty phrases at the silent heavens, cutting themselves with swords and lances, as Elijah taunts them, mocking their so-called god: 'Perhaps he is asleep?' (1Kgs 18:27). Jesus warns against this kind of prayer: 'Do not babble, as the pagans do, they think that they will be heard for their many words' (Mt 6:7). Prayer is not bombarding God with our requests – struggling, with an avalanche of words or pious formulas, to bend his will to ours. In the Carmelite tradition, prayer is just the opposite: it is surrender to *God's* will. Teresa explains the purpose of all prayer: to bring our will into harmony with God's will.[10]

I am reminded of a scene from the play, *Shadowlands*. 'I pray all the time these days,' says C.S. Lewis. 'If I stopped praying, I think I'd stop living.' 'And God hears your prayer, doesn't He?' the chaplain replies. 'We hear Joy's getting better.' 'Yes,' says Lewis, but adds, 'That's not why I pray, Harry. I pray because I can't help myself. I pray because I'm helpless. I pray because the need flows out of me all the time, waking and sleeping. *It doesn't change God. It changes me.*'[11]

Transforming prayer

Carmelite prayer is an affair of the heart, but it is a transforming prayer: a prayer of the '*new* heart' promised by the prophets: 'I will put my law within them, and I will write it upon their hearts... A new heart I will give you, and a new spirit I will put within you' (Jer 31:33; Ez 36:26). 'Prayer is the life of the new heart,' we are told in the *Catechism of the Catholic Church* (#2697). For Carmelites, this 'new heart' is the 'inner room' where Jesus invites his disciples to pray: 'When you pray, go into your room, shut the door and pray to your Father in secret' (Mt 6:6). Prayer means 'taking time frequently to be *alone* with [God],' Teresa tells us (*Life* 8:5; italics mine). 'The only essential,' explains Edith Stein, 'is that one finds, first of all, a quiet corner in which one can communicate with God as though there were nothing else' (SP, p. 54). This prayer requires extended periods of time, as it did for Jesus. It also demands special conditions: silence, solitude, withdrawal into the secret oratory of a quiet heart. Dietrich Bonhoeffer, the great Lutheran theologian, said: 'Teaching about Christ begins in silence'.[12] So, too, does Carmelite prayer: it is a prolonged and silent communing of love with God in the depths of the heart. The poet James McAuley captures the transforming effect of this quiet prayer of faith:

> Incarnate Word, in whom all nature lives,
> Cast flame upon the earth: raise up contemplatives

Among us, men who walk within the fire
Of ceaseless prayer, impetuous desire.
Set pools of silence in this thirsty land...
Prayer has an influence we cannot mark,
It works unseen like radium in the dark.[13]

Dark nights

The challenge on the peaks of Carmel is radical: there can be no compromise with false gods. Elijah calls the wavering people to conversion. They must learn that God is 'turning back their hearts' (1Kgs 18:37). And so the drama unfolds. But the same prophet who urges others to conversion must himself in turn also experience conversion. He withdraws into solitude, impelled by the fury of a woman scorned. In flight from the infamous Jezebel, he journeys into the desert – and into himself – tracing in reverse the exodus experience of the people of God. Here, we are about to see that Elijah was merely human after all, 'as frail as ourselves' in the words of the apostle James (5:17). In the wilderness he sounds the depths of human weakness. He enters a spiritual night and sits desolate amid the debris that was, he feels, his life's achievement: 'It is enough; now, O Lord, take away my life; for I am no better than my fathers' (1Kgs 19:4). This language from such a great prophet and man of prayer may seem to us a kind of false humility. But let me recall a similar, more recent experience. It is recorded in the life of Thérèse of Lisieux.

She, too, experienced abandonment by God in what she calls her 'night of nothingness' during the last eighteen months of her life. She was haunted by 'mocking voices', she tells us, tempted to 'suicide' and 'blasphemy', and she teetered, like Elijah, on the brink of despair. In her trial of faith, Thérèse doubted and questioned. She confided to another sister, Thérèse of St Augustine, 'I don't believe in eternal life, it seems to me that after this mortal life there is nothing left... Everything has disappeared for me, love is all I have.'[14] The account of her last days reads like the story of the crucifixion. It leaves the final gasp of Jesus echoing in our ears: 'My God, my God, why…?'

But perhaps nobody has plumbed the depths of God's absence more deeply than John of the Cross. In a passage often taken as his own self-portrait, he explains that such persons 'resemble one who is imprisoned in a dark dungeon, bound hands and feet, and able neither to move nor see nor feel any favor from heaven or earth. They remain in this condition until their spirit is humbled, softened, and purified, until it becomes so delicate, simple, and refined that it can be one with the Spirit of God' (2DN 7:3). This Elijah experience, too, is part of the Carmelite prayer journey.

Elijah experiences the depths to which God can seek out the human spirit to sear it and kindle in it the fire of his love. This is the God of the burning bush at work in the darkness of faith: 'a consuming fire'. The Lord of the covenant, we are told, 'is a devouring fire, a jealous God' (Dt 4:24; cf. Hb 12:29). Layer upon layer of selfishness is peeled away under God's purifying touch which cleanses the spirit like fire that chars and blackens, until the wood finally glows like a living and consuming flame. The temptation to return to the 'fleshpots of Egypt' and abandon prayer is now more pressing than ever. Here, in this dark hole of despair, Elijah is fed by an angel and finally tastes the heavenly 'manna'. This same Elijah, who was always alert to the word of God, is now called to an even deeper listening. Humbled, softened, purified and refined through apparent failure and abandonment by the Lord, he is about to discover a new face of the living God. He journeys, with hope, 'in the strength of that food forty days and forty nights to Horeb' (1Kgs 19:8) – the mountain of the Lord.

'What are you doing here, Elijah?' (1Kgs 19:9.13). It is not as though God were actually seeking information from this frightened prophet about what he is doing. Rather, his query invites Elijah to become conscious of the events that have brought him to Horeb. There is a parallel in Yahweh's question to Adam in the garden: 'Where are you?' (Gn 3:9). God knew perfectly well where Adam was hiding. His question was to heighten in our first parents an awareness of what they had done by eating the forbidden fruit and the consequences of their action. After the question to Elijah, the prophet is then told: 'Go out and stand upon the mountain before the Lord' (1Kgs 19:11). Not in the elements – the wind, the earthquake, the fire – is the Lord to be found, like the God of thunder and lightning and dark cloud on the heights of Carmel, and once before on Sinai (1Kgs 19:11; Ex 19:16; cf. 1Kgs 18:38; Hb 12:18). This is the God of the gentle breeze, a still small voice that speaks in 'the rustling of a light silence' (1Kgs 19:12), literally 'a sound of thin silence', whispering softly with the breath of God.[15] No 'graven image or likeness' can ever represent the transcendent Yahweh of Israel's story. He remains forever an Unknown Stranger who constantly withdraws into the quiet of his own dark mystery. Carmelites are summoned to listen constantly to the word of God in faith, 'pondering the Lord's law day and night', as the heart of the *Rule* enjoins (#10),[16] with words borrowed from the first psalm. The *Rule* continues: 'and keeping watch' in prayer. No wonder Elijah is a model for every Carmelite, called to be alert to the demands of the word in deep contemplative prayer and to be vigilant, like a watch in the night.

Spiritual combat

'Watch and pray,' say both scripture and the Carmelite *Rule*. As his own battle in Gethsemane opens, Jesus twice warns his sleeping disciples, 'Watch and pray, that you may not enter into temptation' (Mt 26:41). The *Rule* reminds us, in the words of Job, that 'life on earth is a time of trial' (#18; Job 7:1). A Carmelite is called to battle for and with the Lord, as Elijah did

– and will do again – against the powers of darkness: for he appears for the last time in the scriptures as a martyr and witness in the final onslaught of Satan (Rev 11:4-13).[17] Teresa describes the action of the devil here and now in anticipation of his final overthrow as subtle, cunning and treacherous, working like 'a noiseless file' (IC I:2:16). The wiles of the evil one are indeed insidious. So, the *Rule* of Carmel calls us to vigilance – here and now – to stay awake – here and now – to pray – here and now – and even to disturb others, if need be, by witness to our values: ready to be rejected, as Elijah was, in challenging the conscience of our times: 'Is it you,' King Ahab greeted Elijah, 'you troubler of Israel?' (1Kgs 18:17).[18]

This is the prophetic element in Carmelite spirituality. The 1977 *Constitutions* of the Discalced Carmelite Brothers highlight the call to announce the word in the spirit of Elijah: 'We uphold him as the inspirer of Carmel and take his prophetic charism as the model of our vocation to hear the word of God deep within ourselves and to share it with others' (pt I, ch. 1, I:2). But prophecy is also about witnessing in prayerful faithfulness to the truth of God's word. 'All my longing was and still is,' wrote Teresa, 'that since He has so many enemies and so few friends that these few friends be good ones' (WP 1:2). The prophet Habakkuk stands on his watchtower and asks the Lord why wickedness abounds. He gets his answer – one that applies to all: 'See how he flags, he whose soul is not at rights, but the upright man will live by his *faithfulness*' (Hab 2:4). For a Carmelite, 'keeping watch in prayer' is 'standing on the watchtower' – always on guard, like Habakkuk; always, like Elijah, standing faithfully before the face of the living God, praying in his words 'that this people may know that you alone are God' (1Kgs 18:37) and prompting others, in the conflict between good and evil, to respond like the people of Elijah's day: 'The Lord, he is God; the Lord, he is God' (1Kgs 18:39).

Contemplation and action

Undoubtedly, Elijah is a man of stunning exploits. He raised a widow's son to life (1Kgs 17:17-24) and slew the prophets of Baal after a mighty contest on Mount Carmel (1Kgs 18:20-40).[19] The episode of Naboth's vineyard affirms Elijah's concern for social justice (1Kgs 21). But this outstanding man of action is primarily a listener: alert, persevering, and attentive to the word of God. We find a recurring pattern in the prophet's life: withdrawal into solitude followed by intense activity – a telling proof of the quiet space Elijah needed for *listening to the word before he proclaimed it* with his mighty deeds in Yahweh's name. Deep contemplative prayer was for Elijah, as it is for Carmelites, the perennial source and spring of all action and ministry. The story of Elijah ends with God's command: 'Go, and return on your way' (1Kgs 19:15). His solitude was not an escape. He was drawn into God only *to go out of himself* and to embrace the service of others again in a whole new way.

Neither does a Carmelite choose solitude to escape the challenge of life. Contemplation leads to action. Prayer is never a selfish flight from the call of duty or from the grind of daily living. In silence, Carmelites listen more intently, and with compassion, to the pain of the world they have left behind, where their hearts continue to live. They return from their 'Tabors' with a heightened awareness of their mission. From the heights of Tabor so conducive to silent and solitary prayer, the disciples of Jesus must not ignore the vast plains lying beneath, with their undulating fields 'already white for the harvest' (Jn 4:35). So, too, Elijah's encounter with God on Horeb is a peak-experience, not a journey's end. Yahweh immediately resumes his dialogue with him: 'Go, and return on your way', and he informs him of his future mission (1Kgs 19:15-18). Elijah returns to the previous theatre of his activity and shares with his people the fruits of a deeper encounter with God.

Elijah's outreach to others extends beyond God's chosen people. His ministry is taken up in the gospels as a foreshadowing of the universal mission of Jesus: 'There were many widows in Israel in the days of Elijah…and Elijah was sent…only to Zarephath, in the land of Sidon, to a woman who was a widow' (Lk 4:25-26; cf. 1Kgs 17:8-24). Then, after his Horeb experience, Elijah is again sent by God on a wider mission: 'You shall anoint Hazael to be king over Syria,' the Lord tells him (1Kgs 19:15), and so the prophet emerges from solitude with a mission far beyond the confines of Israel. Elijah becomes a figure of unity and reconciliation among faiths.[20] So, too, there is a universal dimension to the Carmelite calling that draws encouragement from this example of Elijah. It is essential to all Christian prayer for a church destined to be one, undivided and whole. Jews, Muslims and Christians of all denominations revere Elijah with a common faith in the God which the prophet's name proclaims: '*Eli-Ya-Hu*', meaning, 'Yahweh is my God'. The Carmelite monastery at the place of Elijah's sacrifice on Mount Carmel is still today a sanctuary teeming with pilgrims of the three major world faiths who come to venerate the great prophet on his feastday (July 20th). This common worship stands out in a divided world as a beacon of hope for the universal mission of the Church and the ultimate fulfilment of Jesus' prayer 'that they may all be one' (Jn 17:21).

A new face of God

Elijah appeared unexpectedly; he now disappears again unexpectedly: carried off mysteriously into heaven 'in a chariot with fiery horses' (2Kgs 2:11). There he remains as if waiting to continue his mission. And so, the scene is set for the arrival of another Elijah who will come after him, a prophetic voice 'crying out in the wilderness' and preparing the way for the Messiah. The world into which John the Baptist was born was filled with the thought of Elijah's return, the prophet Malachi providing the classic biblical text for this expectation: 'Behold, I will send you Elijah the prophet before the great and terrible day of the Lord comes' (4:5 (*RSV*); cf. Sir 48:10). The forerunner of the promised Messiah is foretold as the one who will come 'in the spirit and power of Elijah' (Lk 1:17), and he emerges from the desert clothed like him 'with a garment of camel's hair and a leather girdle' (Mt 3:4; cf. 2Kgs 1:8). Similarities between Elijah and the Baptist are striking.

One such parallel is particularly relevant. It helps explain the transformation of the heart at prayer through repeated and ongoing renewal. Both arrive on the scene with a clarion call to conversion, a call for a change of mind and heart. Elijah prays: 'Answer me, O Lord… that the people may know that you are winning back their hearts' (1Kgs 18:37); the Baptist cries out: 'Repent, for the kingdom of heaven is at hand' (Mt 3:2). Yes, both call for conversion – but both in turn must experience their own conversion: an inner transformation, with a new vision of God.

The Baptist warns at first of 'the wrath that is to come… the axe laid to the root… the winnowing fork in his hand… the unquenchable fire' (Mt 3:7.10.12). This is the face of a God of vengeance – the same God who was apparently unmoved when the Kishon river at the foot of Carmel ran red with the blood of slaughtered prophets unfaithful to Elijah's God. Later, imprisoned in his dark dungeon, John is tested in his faith but not 'scandalised'. Like Elijah he is to discover, in his weakness, a new face of God. In prison, he is told that 'the blind see… the lame walk… the lepers are cleansed… the deaf hear… the dead are raised to life… the poor have the good news preached to them' (Mt 11:5). This is not the God he first proclaimed, nor is it the One who thundered fire from heaven on Carmel. It is a tender God, discovered through rejection, imprisonment and a painful inner transformation. He is foreshadowed in the story of Elijah by the gentle breeze in the encounter on Horeb – a God of compassion with a healing touch revealed in the 'gentle' heart of the Word made flesh. This is the God of Carmelite spirituality as described by Thérèse of Lisieux:

> I need a heart burning with tenderness,
> Who will be my support forever,
> Who loves everything in me, even my weakness…
> And who never leaves me day or night…
> I must have a God who takes on my nature
> And becomes my brother and is able to suffer! (PN 23)

Friends of God

Beside Jesus on Tabor stand two of the great Old Testament figures of prayer. In this scene, Moses could easily steal the limelight from his companion Elijah. He was lawgiver and leader of God's people, and his presence on Tabor reaffirms that 'the law was given through Moses, grace and truth came through Jesus Christ' (Jn 1:17). A powerful intercessor with God, he 'stood in the breach before him' (Ps 105:23), suppliant on the mountain with arms aloft, while Joshua defeated the Amalekites through the power of that incessant prayer (Ex 17:8-13). He was the Lord's intimate confidant: 'Yahweh would talk to Moses face to face, as a man talks to his friend' (Ex 33:11; cf. Nb 12:8). The basic disposition of his whole life is fundamental to all prayer: 'He was extremely humble,' we are told, 'the humblest man on earth' (Nb 12:3). An admiring biblical eulogy provides enduring testimony to his life of prayer: 'There was never such a prophet in Israel as Moses, the man whom Yahweh knew face to face' (Dt 34:10). We can easily understand why his towering stature may seem to dwarf the significance of Elijah beside him on Tabor. But Elijah, too, stood before the face of God as a friend of Yahweh, and to overlook his presence would be to miss some of the deeper implications of the scene and its lesson on prayer.

A witness to persevering prayer

The early Church could hardly have been surprised to find the prophet of Carmel with Moses beside Jesus at prayer on Tabor. The prophet Elijah is linked in the gospels with the identity of Jesus himself and his prayer. Jesus is praying alone before he puts this question to his disciples, 'Who do the people say that I am?', and evokes spontaneously the name of the prophet in reply, 'Some...say Elijah' (Lk 9:18-19). Soon afterwards, Jesus has to temper the missionary ardour of his disciples who, borrowing Elijah's words, ask in the spirit of his prayer, 'Shall we call down fire from heaven?' (Lk 9:54; cf. 2Kgs 1:10.12). When Paul disowns the possibility of Israel's final rejection in the plan of salvation, he uses words addressed by God to Elijah: 'I have kept for myself seven thousand men who have not bowed the knee to Baal' (Rm 11:4; cf. 1Kgs 19:18). This same Elijah, 'human being as frail as ourselves' (Jas 5:17), is also recalled by the apostle James: as a permanent witness to the value of determined and persevering prayer despite human weakness: 'The heartfelt prayer of someone upright works very powerfully' (Jas 5:16).

The word of the cross

But there is a conversion and discovery of God through persevering and deepening prayer never dreamt of by seer or prophet. Again, Elijah points the way. Here on Tabor, with Moses, he speaks to the transfigured Jesus at prayer about his passion-resurrection: 'And suddenly there were two men talking to him; they were Moses and Elijah...and they were speaking of his *departure* [*exodon*] which he was to accomplish at Jerusalem' (Lk 9:30-31). The word 'exodus' here has rich biblical connotations. In the story of Elijah, it evokes his desert march for forty days which in turn recalls the exodus path traversed by God's people for forty years in the wilderness, with Moses at their head. Both journeys culminated in a final theophany or manifestation of God on the same mountain: Sinai, also called Horeb. Here on Tabor, however, the 'exodus' refers to the passion-resurrection of Jesus. It is the *new* exodus and is inseparably linked, in our Carmelite tradition, with growth in prayer. We have already seen the theme of *going out* in the poetry of John of the Cross. But there are deeper implications yet.

There can be no intimate communing with God that is not patterned on the death-resurrection of Jesus and plunges us, with him, into the paschal mystery – the dying and the rising, the pain and the dance, the agony and the glory. In prayer, we too must follow the path of the 'exodus' Jesus travelled when 'his hour had come for him to pass out of this world to the Father' (Jn 13:1). The presence of Elijah on Tabor is a constant reminder that every Carmelite is called to stand at the foot of the cross in prayer and to 'look on him whom they have pierced' (Jn 19:37), contemplating in the crucified Jesus the true face of the living God. Elizabeth of the Trinity explains: 'A Carmelite… is a soul who has *gazed on the Crucified*, who has seen Him offering Himself to His Father as a Victim for souls and, recollecting herself in this great vision of the charity of Christ, has understood the passionate love of His soul, and has wanted to give herself as He did!' (L 133).

The glory of loving
The transfiguration is not just a dazzling event from a remote and distant past. It is ever present in the Church, taking place at each moment in the heart of the believer who responds to the heavenly voice on Tabor: 'This is my Son, the Chosen One. Listen to him' (Lk 9:35). In *John*, the inner transformation is a change from darkness to light: 'He who follows me will not walk in darkness, but will have the light of life' (8:12). To listen in prayer is to enter with Elijah and Moses into the 'glory' of Jesus shining through him on Tabor – 'the glory,' Jesus said,

'which you [Father] have given to me in your love for me before the foundation of the world' (Jn 17:24): the ineffable and eternal 'communion with the Father and his Son Jesus Christ' (1Jn 1:3). As we share in this communion of love, there is always an inner change taking place in prayer.

For Paul, this transforming is the creative action of God conforming us 'to the image of his Son' (Rm 8:29). He describes it with the same term used of Jesus on Tabor in *Matthew* (17:2) and *Mark* (9:2) when he says that we 'are being *transfigured* (*metamorphoumetha*) into his likeness'; he further adds that 'this comes from the Lord who is the Spirit' (2Cor 3:18). It is all part of the new creation now groaning continually in the birth pangs of a new heaven and a new earth, promised for the end of time when we shall all be *changed* (cf. 1Cor 15:51). For the moment, however, 'we await a Saviour, the Lord Jesus Christ, who will change our lowly body to be like his glorious body' (Ph 3:20-21). Prayer is an invitation to surrender in advance, here and now, to the searching flame of God's transforming love and to open ourselves, unreservedly, to the refining fire of his gentle touch. Without constant renewal, inner conversion and the surprising disclosures of an ever unfolding mystery of God under the purifying action of the Spirit, there can be no deep prayer.

'Look towards him and be radiant'

To pray is to be with Jesus, to 'look towards him and be radiant' with his glory (Ps 33:6): 'The glory which you have given to me, I have given to them... I desire that those also, whom you have given to me, may be with me where I am in order that they may see my glory' (Jn 17:22.24). To pray *is* to be with Jesus, bathed in his glory – even here on earth. The light of God already shines on us 'all glorious within'. For it is not the visible splendour that matters – the blinding light, the extraordinary manifestation, the spectacular, that sometimes mark the journey of prayer. These may come and go. They did on Tabor. The radiant vision faded and quiet enveloped the scene: 'They kept silence and told no one,' we are told (Lk 9:36). What matters most is the inner transformation of the heart, the love that burns in the ordinary, the humdrum, the grinding monotony of persevering prayer – the darkness of faith in Jesus: 'It is the God who said, "Let light shine out of darkness" who has shone in our hearts to give the light of the knowledge of the glory of God in the face of Christ' (2Cor 4:6). Moses veiled his face as it shone with the glory of God on Sinai, and Elijah wrapped his face in his mantle as the Lord passed by on Horeb (Ex 34:33.35; 1Kgs 19:13). But 'we all, with unveiled faces, reflecting the glory of the Lord as in a mirror, are being transfigured into his likeness from one degree of glory to another' (2Cor 3:18). After all the dazzling glory of Tabor, Jesus was once again 'the carpenter, the son of Mary… Jesus of Nazareth, the son of Joseph' (Mk 6:3; Jn 1:45; cf. Jn 6:42) – to all appearances just an ordinary man, fully human: 'they saw no one with them any more, but only Jesus' (Mk 9:8) – *only* Jesus. He is the focus of all Carmelite prayer. Jesus alone!

'What I say to you I say to all'

Thomas Merton once wrote: 'There is no member of the Church who does not owe something to Carmel.'[21] But I believe we can go even further and say that Carmelite spirituality answers to the deepest need for love in every human heart. Witness the final chorus of *Les Misérables*:

> Do you hear the people sing lost in the valley of the night?
> It is the music of a people who are climbing to the light.
> For the wretched of the earth there is a flame that never dies.
> Even the darkest night will end and the sun will rise.[22]

Here we catch an echo of the *Song of Songs*:

> Love is strong as Death,
> passion as relentless as Sheol.
> The flash of it is a flash of fire,
> a flame of Yahweh himself. (8:6)

Carmel is all about that flame. It is sometimes experienced as painful in the purifying action of the Holy Spirit – God's searching fire – and testing in the darkness of faith. But it is never extinguished. John of the Cross calls it the 'Living Flame of Love'.

This lesson of Carmel's universal appeal I was to learn on a visit to Taizé. There, in the vast tent of reconciliation, lights flickered before an icon. The rest was darkness. There were none of the trappings of structured religion: statues, paintings or church candles. People had space and time for silence. They really prayed – people of all religions and, perhaps even more importantly, people of no religion at all. I had long savoured those haunting Taizé chants but, on this occasion, it was the words of one particular mantra that struck me most. They were very familiar to me, taken from the *Bookmark* of Teresa: '*Nada te turbe*... let nothing trouble you.' Then another mantra. This, too, had a distinct Carmelite flavour: 'Within our darkest night you kindle a fire that never dies away.' Over and over again, I heard the refrain: 'Watch and pray, watch and pray.' The music faded off into silence, quiet and stillness. Taizé, too, draws inspiration from Elijah; it is alive with resonances of the great prophet:

> Not in the whirlwind, not in the lightning,
> not in the strife of tongues is [God] to be found,
> but in the still, small voice, speaking in silence.
> Therefore be silent...
> Be still and know.[23]

I discovered that Taizé was simply reaffirming Carmel's ancient message for thirsting hearts today: 'Watch and pray... Watch and pray... Be still and know.'

Notes

1 An earlier version of this chapter was delivered as a talk to the students of Mansfield College, Oxford on February 5th, 2003.

2 On the origins of the Order, see ch. 3, note 10.

3 '[Our predecessors] tarried long in the solitude of the desert, conscious of their own imperfection. Sometimes, however, though rarely, they came down from their desert, anxious, so as not to fail in what they regarded as their duty, to be of service to their neighbours, and sowed broadcast of the grain, threshed out in preaching, that they had so sweetly reaped in solitude with the sickle of contemplation.': see Nicholas of Narbonne, *The Flaming Arrow*, Durham: Teresian Press, 1985, VI:17-18, p. 30.

4 For a competent survey of the various interpretations of the *Rule* – in relation to Elijah – from its origin until the present day, see Jane Ackerman, *Elijah: Prophet of Carmel*, Washington, DC: ICS Publications, 2003.

5 See chapter 3 for a fuller discussion of the Carmelite *Rule*.

6 The inspiration of Elijah for the Order of Carmel was first stated in its Constitutions of 1281: in the opening lines, now known as the *Rubrica Prima*. This was the Carmelites' first recorded attempt at defining their identity, and their conviction appeared in the opening paragraphs of constitution after constitution for hundreds of years; see Ackerman, *op. cit.*, pp. 122-3. For a helpful discussion of the Carmelite Order's search for identity, see Wilfrid McGreal, OCarm, *At the Fountain of Elijah: The Carmelite Tradition*, London: Darton, Longman & Todd, 1999, pp. 37-48.

7 Ackerman treats well the relevance, the difficulties and the challenge of the ancient prophet Elijah for present-day readers of his story: see Ackerman, *op. cit.*, pp. 1-31. See also Kilian Healy, OCarm, *Prophet of Fire*, Rome: Institutum Carmelitanum, 1990.

8 A recent issue of *Mount Carmel* covers the many and various aspects of Elijah's story and their relation to the Carmelite charism: see *Mount Carmel*, vol. 51/3, 2003.

9 'For the Lord in speaking to Saint Elijah speaks to every monk and hermit, of the old and of the new Law: *Depart from here*, namely

from the frail and fleeting things of this world; *and go eastward,* away, that is, from the lusts your flesh is heir to; *and hide yourself by the brook Cherith,* dwelling no more in cities with the multitude; *that is over against the Jordan,* so that you may thus be divided from your sins by charity. Ascending then by these four steps to the pinnacle of prophetic perfection, *there you shall drink from the brook.* And so that you may persevere upon this way, *I have commanded the ravens to feed you there.*': see *The Book of the Institution of the First Monks (Chapters 1 to 9),* Oxford: Teresian Press, 1969, ch. 2, p. 5. For the influence of this work, often known simply as *The Institution,* on the development of the whole Carmelite tradition, see Ackerman, *op. cit.,* pp. 141-79. McGreal writes: 'After the Rule it is possibly the key work in any understanding of Carmelite spirituality and certainly from 1400 onwards dominated the Carmelites' historical thinking and their vision of the Order.': see McGreal, *op. cit.,* pp. 38-9.

10   'The highest perfection obviously does not consist in interior delights or in great raptures or in visions or in the spirit of prophecy but in having our will so much in conformity with God's will that there is nothing we know He wills that we do not want with all our desire' (F 5:10).

11   William Nicholson, *Shadowlands: A Play,* London: Samuel French, 1990, Act II, p. 41; italics mine.

12   See Dietrich Bonhoeffer, *Christology,* London: Collins / New York: Harper & Row, 1966, p. 27.

13   From 'A Letter to John Dryden', in James McAuley, *Collected Poems 1936-1970,* Sydney: Angus & Robertson, 1971, p. 94.

14   Quoted in PN, p. 184. See also her words to her sister Marie: 'I *count only on love*' (LT 242).

15   In a splendid article, Craig E. Morrison outlines the various suggested translations of this rich phrase: see 'Handing on the Mantle: The Transmission of the Elijah Cycle in the Biblical Versions', in Keith J. Egan, T. OCarm & Craig E. Morrison, OCarm (eds), *Master of the Sacred Page: Essays and Articles in Honor of Roland E. Murphy, O.Carm., on the Occasion of his Eightieth Birthday,* Washington, DC: The Carmelite Institute, 1997, pp. 109-29 (especially pp. 112-8).

16   Reference to the *Rule* follows the numbering of points as agreed by the OCarm and OCD General Councils: see Joseph Chalmers, OCarm & Camilo Maccise, OCD, 'On the Citation of the

Carmelite Rule in Official Documents', January 30th, 1999, in John Malley, Camilo Maccise & Joseph Chalmers, *In Obsequio Jesu Christi: The Letters of the Superiors General O.Carm. and O.C.D. 1992-2002*, Rome: Edizioni OCD, 2003, pp. 125-39.

17 'According to the testimony of the Book of Revelation, [Elijah] will return near the end of the world to suffer a martyr's death for his Lord in the battle against the Antichrist.': see Edith Stein, HL, p. 3.

18 Compare the *Jerusalem Bible* translation: 'you scourge of Israel'. For a discussion of the *Rule* and spiritual combat, see ch. 3, section 'Community'.

19 The main purpose of Elijah in this episode was not to shed the blood of these false prophets – a gesture comprehensible only within the religious framework of the time – but the conversion of the people. This incident must never be used to justify slaughter or even intolerance directed, in the name of God, against people at variance with our beliefs and convictions; see *A Biblical Prayer Journey in the Holy Land, op. cit.*, p. 391. Ackerman comments: 'For centuries readers have remembered and retold the most dramatic parts of [Elijah's] old story, such as the holocaust on Mt Carmel or Elijah's ascension into heaven. However, in his oldest tale found in *1-2 Kings*, what matters most about Elijah are the results of such powerful experiences, not the spectacular events themselves. These and everything else in that story knit his people to God.': see Ackerman, *op. cit.*, p. 31.

20 Competently and with a wealth of scholarship and detail, Ackerman outlines Elijah's role in the three great faiths of Judaism, Christianity and Islam: see Ackerman, *op. cit.*, ch. 2, 'The Prophet in Later Legends', pp. 35-75, and ch. 3, 'Elijah and the Spiritual Life', pp. 77-111. See also the important collections of essays on Elijah in scripture, Christian and non-Christian traditions and the Carmelite charism: Bruno de Jésus-Marie, OCD (ed.), *Élie le prophète*, 2 vols, Paris: Desclée de Brouwer, 1956; Paul Chandler, OCarm (ed.), *A Journey with Elijah*, Rome: Institutum Carmelitanum, 1991.

21 Thomas Merton, *The Ascent to Truth*, London: Hollis & Carter, 1951, p. ix.

22 Lyrics of the 'Finale' by Alain Boublil, Herbert Kretzmer & Jean-Marc Natel; music by Claude-Michel Schönberg.

23 Attributed to the writings of Taizé; quoted in *Mount Carmel*, vol. 48/3, 2000, p. 45.

Chapter 3

The Carmelite Rule:
A Gospel Approach[1]

The three-layered approach

A distinction given by Vatican II for a better understanding of the origin of the gospels[2] is a perfect starting-point for exploring the potential for spiritual growth embedded in the Carmelite *Rule*. We can distinguish three stages in the formation of the gospels:

1. What Jesus did and taught prior to the ascension. This is the Christ-event: the *Jesus* of time and space and his *message* in the historical context of his life and death. This first stage is Christ-centred.

2. The handing on (tradition, both oral and written) of the Christ-event in the light of the *deepening and lived experience* of it by the early Christian community, enlightened by the Spirit, and prior to the writing of the gospels. This second stage is community-centred.

3. Documents written with the *evangelists' personal slant* and creative expression of the Christ-event. Drawing on what was handed on (tradition, both oral and written), the authors 'selected, synthesised and drew out the implications' in response to a concrete community situation.[3] Their records are carefully shaped by an original insight. This third stage is written documents-centred.

These three stages are inseparably linked to each other and entirely interdependent.[4] If we do not see the gospels in this way, we run the risk of a purely factual or fundamentalist approach to the word of God, with everything taken literally; or of seeing the developing gospel tradition as a mere creation of the early Christian community, without roots in the historical Jesus. Both extremes must be avoided.[5]

Contexts

The Word became flesh in a specific, historical context, conditioned in time and space. It is easy from the pages of the gospels to recreate – at least in broad outline – the world into which Jesus was born, with its Semitic language and culture (Aramaic); its imagery, pastoral (sheep, goats, birds, seeds, flowers) and urban (traders, merchants, money, taxes); its idioms (allegory, parable, metaphor, discourse, narrative); its landscape of undulating hills and mountains (Golan, Hebron, Judea, Negev), dotted with towns, large (Capernaum, Bethsaida) and small (Nazareth, Bethlehem); its meandering river (Jordan), inland sea (Lake Galilee) and fertile plain (Jezreel).[6] The social milieu, too, opens up to the keen and observant gospel reader – its political conflicts (freedom-fighters, zealots against tyrannical Rome); religious movements (Sadducees and Pharisees); festal celebrations (Passover, Tabernacles); and a motley assortment of inhabitants (poor, rich, widows, tax-collectors, blind, lame and beggars).[7]

All these are part of so many layers that may have to be peeled away in order to reach the truth enfleshed in Jesus and first proclaimed in one confined part of the world, a teaching destined to spread to the ends of the earth until the close of time and still needing to be incarnated among so many diverse peoples. We call this process *inculturation*, with Jesus and his message always central to it – a whole dynamic process, long, painful and risky. Not for the faint-hearted, the narrow, the closed mindset. But absolutely essential for any community journeying, like the early Christians, into the unknown and open to the work of the Spirit. It is the exodus mentality.

Like the gospels, the Carmelite *Rule*, too, has its own historical context, conditioned as it is in space and time.[8] We find it embedded in a geographical setting similar to that of the gospels and reflecting the political, social and religious concerns of the late twelfth to early thirteenth century. It is a rule of the Holy Land.[9] It has come down to us enhanced by associations with Elijah and the schools of the prophets on Mount Carmel and enriched by its association with the wadi 'Ain es Siah where the Order was born.[10] That remote solitary range, with its secluded valley, was ideal for the first hermits. However, driven later from this idyllic setting by the advancing Saracens from 1238 onwards, and with the expansion of the Order as a result to Europe and later even further afield, Carmelites would be forced to discover in every place a 'spiritual' Carmel – an inner solitude, silence and prayer of the heart – in the midst of busy towns and cities.

Many of the first hermits were themselves crusaders impelled by religious fervour to recapture the Holy City from infidel hands. The *Rule* abounds in martial imagery – breastplate, shield, helmet, sword, arrows, cincture – drawn from the *Letter to the Ephesians* (6:11-17). This extensive use of a warrior's panoply provided Western warlike soldiers with a meaningful vocabulary for the 'trial' and 'persecution' of the spiritual combat mentioned in the *Rule* (#18). Even the replacement of the Pauline 'obedience' to Christ[11] with the term 'allegiance' (*obsequium*) to him (#2) is evocative of the feudal system widespread in the Palestine of the *Rule* – 'allegiance' from 'ad', meaning 'towards', and 'liege', meaning 'feudal lord' or sovereign of vassal subjects. This same phrase profoundly characterised medieval Christianity at the time of the crusades.[12] In the *Rule*, however, there is no suggestion of *slavish surrender* redolent of *blind* or *unquestioning* obedience, even to Christ. The document allows for both dialogue and community discussion (#15) which are attuned to a more nuanced understanding of obedience. Both of these are envisaged in the *Rule.*

Another example of historical context: the *Rule* is a male document, written by a man for men. It would be more than two hundred years before women were admitted to the Order (1452). Some more sensitive accommodation to the concerns of women today may be required.[13] An Order of the *Brothers* of Our Lady of Mount Carmel could possibly reflect more explicitly in some way the presence of *Sisters,* too, by the use of inclusive language.

The *Rule* also emerges out of the maelstrom of political conflicts of the day between the warring Saracen and Christian faiths. The assassination in 1214 of Albert, the Latin patriarch and author of the *Rule,* and his residence in Acre rather than in Jerusalem which was then under Muslim control, bear telling witness to those turbulent times in which the *Rule* was written.

Christocentric

The *Rule* of Carmel, like the gospels, is christocentric. It is the pervasive use of scripture that seems for the most part to make it so.[14] 'The new is hidden in the old,' Augustine wrote, 'and the old is made manifest in the new', while Jerome wrote, 'Ignorance of the scriptures is ignorance of Christ'.[15] Conversely, to know and love the scriptures is to know and love Christ. Albert is one who speaks and thinks explicitly in biblical terms, and the document itself is a mosaic of biblical texts; as said earlier, it reflects the style of a discourse from *Matthew* even more than that of a legal document. Scripture quotations abound, explicit and implicit, at first sight apparently disproportionate in our *Rule* which is the most diminutive among its peers.

In its extensive use of biblical quotations, the *Rule* is following the tradition of St Basil, exemplified in his *Moralia*, the collection of scriptural sentences that forms the basis of his own *Rule*. He did not include one word of his own, believing that any human addition would be superfluous to the word of God. Still more radically than Basil, the desert fathers refused to have a rule altogether, fearing that it would foster servile observance characteristic of the old law and thus preclude the freedom of the gospel; hence their decision to preserve their charism not by laws but by living examples.[16] Likewise, the first Carmelites began by being themselves a living rule – indeed, a *living word*.

'The word of God,' we are told, 'must abound in your mouths and hearts' (#19). And anticipating the words of Vatican II – that 'prayer should accompany the reading of sacred Scripture'[17] – the *Rule* continues, 'Let all you do have the Lord's word for accompaniment' (#19). Littered with scripture texts, the document disposes the Carmelite, mind and heart, to be saturated with Christ's presence through his word. The focus of such prayer is 'pondering the Lord's law' (#10) – that is, the word; a 'listening together…to a reading from Holy Scripture' is prescribed for mealtimes (#7); the assurance that 'holy meditation will save you' is also there (#19; Prov 2:11); a reminder that 'the sword of the Spirit [is] the word of God' (#19) comes with an explicit reference to what 'our Lord says in the gospel' (#21) and to the inspired teaching of Paul 'into whose mouth,' we are told, 'Christ put his own words' (#20; cf. 2Cor 13:3). This apostle, in turn, is quoted explicitly at length with a glowing endorsement of work through his own example, 'toiling night and day', and with a warning against 'restless idlers' (#20; cf. 2Th 3:7-12).

But perhaps even more significant than all this, the person of Christ embraces the whole document. Apart from several explicit references to Christ throughout, the initial greeting, 'health in the Lord' (#1), is followed immediately by an implicit reference to *Hebrews* with the words, 'many and varied…ways' (#2; Hb 1:1), evoking God's final and definitive revelation in his Son. This, in turn, is followed by a description of religious life – indeed of the vocation common to all the baptised – as essentially a following of Christ.[18] The *Rule* gradually unfolds, and the typically Carmelite prayer of 'pondering the Lord's law day and night' (#10) is directed implicitly to the person of Christ who replaces the law (cf. Jn 1:17); the next phrase, 'keeping watch at his prayers', further opens up implicitly a perspective on the return of Christ. The movement then comes back full circle again from Christ at the end to Christ at the beginning, with a large inclusion bracketing and uniting the whole document: the *Rule* concludes explicitly evoking the *parousia*: 'our Lord, at his second coming' (#24). In addition, the prescription, unknown to the ancient desert monks, for a daily celebration of mass binds the religious into one, a living community gathered around the eucharistic Lord (#14).

Hence, the importance of the first preliminary stage in the formation of the gospels for a better understanding of the Carmelite *Rule* as essentially christocentric. And the need to strip it, where necessary, of archaic dress, outdated structures and the spatial limitations of a historically conditioned document, if the core message of Carmel is to extend like the gospels and take root through *inculturation* in a vast variety of places and times.

Community

But there is much to be learnt, too, from the second stage in the formation of the gospels for a better understanding of the *Rule*: the focus on community. The Church is a living community in *Acts* growing, under the action of the Spirit, in its understanding of Jesus. There we see the essential traits of an ideal early Christian community. Vatican II has restored their fresh vision of Church by shifting the emphasis from a pyramid, triangle or hierarchical structure back to its self-understanding as *communio*.[19] The evangelists give expression to this early community lifestyle, already existing before the gospels themselves were written.

So, too, with the *Rule* of Carmel. It gives a legal framework at the request of the first Carmelites to their specific way of life which was already a lived community experience, or charism, before ever it was codified in writing – 'a rule of life [*formula vitae*],' we are told, 'in keeping with your avowed purpose [*propositum*]' or plan (#3). The lawgiver of Carmel is clearly inspired by the Jerusalem model of the Church in the early chapters of *Acts*: the sharing and friendship; the joy, freedom, openness and dialogue; the listening to the word – a multi-faceted Church of varied charisms and ministries, pulsating with the breath of the Spirit impelling it to growth and expansion.

Even a cursory glance at *Acts* confirms these observations. There the community is united 'mind and heart' in the bond of mutual love (Acts 4:32). This primacy of love is everywhere affirmed. The believers were united in this way because 'they devoted themselves to the apostles' teaching and fellowship, to the breaking of bread and the prayers' (2:42). These virtues emerge as basic and perennial Christian values. They are reaffirmed of the community a second time in *Acts*: 'Attending the temple together and breaking bread in their homes... praising God' (2:46-47).

But the ideal of the early Christian community is no starry-eyed vision. Some of the early hermits came to the Holy Land as penitent pilgrims. Others were warring crusaders. For these, the recapture of an earthly Jerusalem was to give way to the conquest of a heavenly one. The way forward was still beset with obstacles and called for vigilance, perseverance and defensive weapons. Albert quotes *Job*: 'man's life on earth is a time of trial'

(#18; Job 7:1). This requires spiritual weapons, for the devil is always 'on the prowl like a roaring lion,' the *Rule* reminds us, echoing Peter (#18; 1Pet 5:8). So, the *Letter to the Ephesians* on the spiritual combat is taken up again in the *Rule* with striking relevance: 'clothe yourselves in God's armour' (#18; Eph 6:11). The Carmelite community, like the early Christian community, is a fragile one in need of God's weaponry which Albert insists must, in Paul's expression, be *put on.*[20] Our defences, then, are God's gift; he clothes the community with his own strength.

'Faith' is the 'shield' for all occasions, without which 'there can be no pleasing God,' we are told; and hope of salvation is the 'helmet' providing the basis for trust (#19). This armour of God is in turn at the service of *communio*, directing the Carmelite, the *Rule* says, 'to love the Lord your God with all your heart and soul and strength and your neighbour as yourself' (#19; cf. Dt 6:5; Mt 19:19; 22:37-39). In this relentless battle, then, the theological virtues of faith, hope and love are God's armour – his powers – and take pride of place. Carmelite asceticism is primarily God's work, not ours. But it is also closely linked with human endeavour. Albert insists on 'work'; it comprises more than one third of the *Rule*. He further links it with silence, which again enhances *communio*: 'Sin will not be wanting where there is much talk' (#21; Prov 10:19). The Carmelite is to 'watch and pray' (cf. #10) – a phrase in the *Rule* evoking the Gethsemane scene: 'Watch and pray that you may not enter into temptation' (Mk 14:38). 'Watch and pray' – alert, vigilant and always ready to brandish the weapons of God in defence of the common life. Admonished in this way both by scripture and the *Rule*, the Carmelite is called to *put on the armour of God* like a sentinel on guard, to remain *constant in faith*, to keep kindled *the flame of love* in community and to *rely in hope* on the promise of a heavenly Jerusalem.

Two further points of contact between the cenobitical Carmelite lifestyle and the early Church community might be worth mentioning. We recall that in the Jerusalem community 'no one claimed private ownership of any possessions, as everything they owned was held in common' (Acts 4:32). From communion of hearts within that community flowed a common sharing of goods, without social distinction or divisive self-interest. Such is the spiritual demand of radical poverty required of those united 'mind and heart'. The *Rule* of Carmel, too, enjoins renunciation of possessions as an exercise of *communio* in almost identical terms: 'None of the brothers must lay claim to anything as his own, but you are to possess everything in common' (#12; cf. Acts 4:32; 2:44). The radical poverty of the *Rule* is an expression of fraternal sharing in love.

Albert, like the author of *Acts*, gives prominence to the eucharist – for him, a focal point in the community; to prayerful listening with the scriptures – making Christ present; and to prayer – with its still-point in the person of Jesus who embodies 'a new law', replacing the literal 'law' of the Lord in the *Rule*: an inner law written on human hearts by the Spirit of the living God (2Cor 3:3). We might add, with reference to the Our Father recommended in the *Rule* (#11), that it is a 'compendium of the whole gospel' and of 'heavenly doctrine'.[21] Moreover, for Teresa this same prayer contains 'the entire spiritual way' (WP 42:5), a point also stressed by John of the Cross who said that all the Church's prayer is 'reducible to the *Pater Noster*' (3A 44:4). To pray the Our Father is to praise and petition God with the mind and heart of an ecclesial community, children addressing *our* (rather than *my*) Father. It is reassuring to find all three elements – scripture, eucharist and silent prayer – in Albert's vision for his new community. These are values that give a distinctive stamp to our Carmelite life.

Such a lifestyle embodied in the *Rule* highlights the importance of the second preliminary stage in the formation of the gospels for a better understanding of Carmelite life as essentially community-centred – modelled on the shared communion of the early Church, and already a lived experience before it was ever a written document.

Written word

Likewise, there is much to be learnt from the third stage in the formation of the gospels for a better understanding of the *Rule*: the focus on a written document shaped by an original insight. The gospels have their own special literary form. So, too, has the *Rule*. It follows the contemporary literary form of a Letter[22] – a standard framework giving ample scope for considerable flexibility of content and variation of people addressed. It is directed not just to Brocard,[23] but also to 'whoever may succeed you as Prior' (#22) and is a legal document. Albert was well versed in juridical matters; he was also thoroughly informed about the then current movements of religious life. And so, the Patriarch of Jerusalem was admirably equipped to write the *Rule*.

The gospels are an intricate web of diverse strands of tradition, oral and written, fused deftly into what appears, at first sight, a seamless robe. So, too, Albert's *Rule* is interwoven with traditions that already preceded and shaped it, although these are never expressly mentioned in the text. The reference to 'the spring of Elijah' (#1) evokes a long oral tradition centred on the prophet of Mount Carmel, who is now in a real sense father and founder for all Carmelites, wishing to live in his spirit.

The text is also influenced by the *Rule* of Augustine (the rule followed by the Canons Regular of the Holy Cross of whom Albert was one) and by the *Rule* of Benedict, with its monastic tradition. 'Our saintly forefathers' mentioned in the Carmelite *Rule* (#2.11) would have embraced such classical spiritual authors as Cassian (his *Conferences*), Basil and Jerome. Albert, however, did not adopt any of the already existing rules. He opted for a new contemporary concept – a way of life between the monastic orders and the laity. So, the *Rule* bears its own original stamp and is a creative expression of a new form of religious life.

This new lifestyle already existed, with its own inner life of growth, development, expansion and adaptation before the *Rule* gave it legal form. The definitive document emerged from an intensely lived experience of Carmelites striving to discover their own identity during the first forty years of their history. We can trace the successive stages of their search in the *Rule*. First, they were *hermits living solitary lives* in the wadi 'Ain es Siah under their leader Brocard, occupying separate cells, reflecting on scripture and devoting themselves to prayer. Later, they became *hermits living in community* under a prior, with structures to preserve their common sharing of the eucharist, food and other goods. Finally, through forced expansion to Europe and through changed circumstances, they opted for the lifestyle of *mendicant friars*, with ministries such as preaching and the public celebration of the eucharist. These three strands of religious lifestyle have spawned family tensions and conflicts down the ages, but they are inseparably linked at the deepest level of what it means to be a true Carmelite. Albert achieved a balanced and harmonious blend of all three. In this lies the originality of his *Rule*.

Eremitical lifestyle

The stress on the eremitical aspect emerges clearly – prayer, keeping vigil, silence, solitude, separate cells, pondering the scriptures.[24] Their ultimate purpose is inner transformation. The Carmelite is called to be a *hermit at heart*. Such is the deeper dimension of the *Rule*. At the outset, Albert directs the Carmelite to Jesus Christ and faithful service of him 'pure in heart' (#2). The word *heart*[25] already opens up an inner space where the exercises and safeguards of the solitary life take on depth and purpose. Listening to the scriptures allows 'the sword of the Spirit, the word of God' to penetrate the deep heart's core (#19). The solitary allows the word to question experience, and experience in turn to question the word. Carmelites are called to know the scriptures from the inside: 'the word of God must abound in your mouths and hearts' (#19; cf. Col 3:16; Rm 10:8).

Consider the originality of Albert's stress on silence. Within the tradition of religious life, there is no other rule which reserves, comparatively speaking, so much space for silence. It is indicative of Albert's insight. The legislator who is so succinct elsewhere is expansive here. The four basic exercises surrounding the cell are described in two lines: remaining, pondering, watching, praying (#10). But silence has two hundred and ninety-nine words devoted to it, while faith, hope and love have only seventy-two. Moreover, Albert is astute in his choice of scripture texts throughout the *Rule* – selecting, synthesising and drawing out their implications (to borrow the terms of Vatican II about the task of the evangelists).[26] Nowhere, perhaps, is he more discreet and discerning than in the cluster of scripture texts he chooses in support of silence (#21; e.g. Is 32:17; Sir 20:8; Mt 12:36). All of these stress the spiritual combat, with a view to intimacy and quiet communion alone with God.

But the heart of the eremitical life is not silence in itself; silence is the atmosphere that must envelop it. Neither is it the cell. We are not just dealing with a material dwelling-place; the cell is the visible symbol of an inner shrine with space for God. The *Rule* rightly exhorts: 'your *breast* [must be] fortified by holy meditations' (#19). At the centre of the empty room is the risen Christ and a Spirit-filled pray-er focused on the word in quiet expectation of the second coming: 'pondering the Lord's law day and night and keeping watch' (#10). The eremitical aspect of the *Rule* bears the stamp of Albert's original touch.

Cenobitical lifestyle

Since Vatican II, a renewed understanding of community in terms of interpersonal relationships has been paramount.[27] This, as we shall now see, is reflected in the *Rule*. It also helps us to discern some specific characteristics of Carmelite community which highlight the shift from a dominantly eremitical lifestyle to a newly emerging cenobitical one.

This life in common is to be leavened by prayer, scripture reading, solitude and silence – all typical of the eremitical life. But there is also *work* to be done in common, for the most part in silence, while preserving the bond of love. This new family of friends will work from within the word of God: 'Let all you do have the Lord's word for accompaniment,' says the *Rule* (#19; cf. Col 3:17; 1Cor 10:31).

The emphasis on the community leader as 'Prior' (#4.9.12.22.23) has considerable significance. He is not an abbot, for example, who is chosen for life. He is a *brother among brothers*. His role is described in gospel terms as a loving service of others – a superior, we are told, who makes Christ present in the community: 'Whoever pays you heed pays heed to me' (#23; Lk 10:16).

In the midst of the cells there is to be a common oratory bringing the community together for the daily celebration of mass (#14). All the separate cells are thus united, through mutual bonds of love, into a temple of living stones built around a eucharistic presence at the centre of the community. A common refectory, too, is prescribed where the religious are to gather for a shared meal and prayerful listening to the scriptures (#7).[28] Besides this, 'the indiscretions and failings of the brothers... should be lovingly corrected' in a common gathering (#15).

There is a specific community dimension to the panoply of spiritual defences in the *Letter to the Ephesians*, from which Albert borrows copiously. The reference to the 'cincture' in the armour of God is recalled implicitly in the *Rule* using the words of scripture: 'Your loins are to be girt' (#19; Eph 6:14). The 'girded loins' evoke the expectant watchfulness of a soldier on guard. This ties in admirably with the end-time perspective in Albert's stress on 'keeping watch' in prayer (#10). But the image also comes to us rich in connotations of the exodus meal to be eaten 'with a girdle round your waist' (Ex 12:11). It evokes the vision of a praying Carmelite community in exile on a collective pilgrimage, faced with obstacles and difficulties but determined to share in the victory of the new passover.[29] The imagery would have had special significance for many of the first hermits who came as pilgrims to the Holy Land, eventually to settle on Mount Carmel; there they continued the penitential life on which they had already embarked while in Europe, as part of the movement known as 'The Poor of Christ'.[30] This imagery would, in turn, take on additional significance when the first community was later exiled from the Holy Land.

It is worth noting, however, that the *Rule* has no reference to the soldier's 'footwear', also mentioned in the spiritual armour of *Ephesians* (6:15). A mention of these 'shoes… bringing the gospel of peace' might easily be seen to open a perspective as yet foreign to Carmelite life at this earlier stage of its development. Albert's *Rule* could have been misconstrued because of it, in terms of Isaiah's words: 'How beautiful upon the mountains are the feet of the messenger who brings good news and announces peace!' (Is 52:7). This would be a premature interpretation, implying that behind the first *hermits living in community* there were evangelists, with feet shod in readiness to proclaim the gospel worldwide in the spirit of the mendicant orders. Only later did Innocent IV, with his definitive approval of the *Rule* in 1247, give the mendicant spirit its official place in the Carmelite charism. To this aspect of the *Rule* we now turn our attention.

Mendicant lifestyle

A comparison of the original text (1206-14) with the later one, 'corrected, emended, and confirmed' by Innocent IV (1247), highlights subsequent redactions of Albert's *Rule* – omissions, additions, relaxations and improvements – in the light of changing circumstances. The earlier version was a flexible text open to growth, movement and the new life-experiences of the community. We should read the definitive *Rule* too with the same spirit, open in our approach to the charism it enshrines, ever searching for a deeper understanding of it and always ready to adapt to new needs and changing conditions. Albert prescribes fasting, but with the clause: '*unless* [for] bodily sickness or feebleness, or some other good reason' (#16). His apparently stringent requirement, 'You are *always* to abstain from meat, except as a remedy for sickness or *excessive* feebleness' (#17), is later modified by Innocent IV who dropped both the 'always' and the 'excessive'. To this we can add the permission granted in the definitive *Rule*: 'when you are on a journey… you may eat foodstuffs that have been cooked with meat… At sea, however, meat may be eaten' (#17) – a mitigation which pointedly describes the changed situation of the Carmelites with new foundations abroad and the necessity of travel by sea. These modifications and mitigations are an application of the *Rule*'s more general principle for the distribution of common goods to each religious according to 'whatever befits his age and needs' (#12); likewise, 'need is not bound by law' (#16).

We have a highly significant exception to the instruction on remaining in the cell, which Albert tempered by: '*unless* attending to some other duty' (#10). This 'duty', literally 'lawful activities' ('*iustis occasionibus*'), is not specified. But it must surely qualify as *work*, explicitly referred to a few paragraphs later: 'You must give yourself to work of some kind, so that the devil may always find you busy' (#20). Again, the work is unspecified. But the emphasis on work is endorsed by Innocent's addition and conclusion to the whole section: 'That is the way of holiness and goodness: see that you follow it'

(#20). We have here an important stress on being occupied, in contrast to being idle. So we find, already in embryo, the later extension of 'lawful activities' to the ministry of mendicant friars. Not that this was a quantum leap: even the reactionary and uncompromising Nicholas ('the Frenchman') of Narbonne, author of *The Flaming Arrow*, had to concede that the hermits on Mount Carmel went out to preach from time to time![31]

Forced to return to Europe, the Carmelites resonated with the mendicant movement. The *Rule's* accent shifted to embrace the demands of a new ministry in view of a different culture. Innocent's reduction of the night-silence from 'after Vespers until Terce' to 'after Compline until after Prime' (#21) was most likely an accommodation to the pressing demands of this new lifestyle. The point of gravity in the new society had shifted from the countryside to the cities. This was part of the 'signs of the times' and called for adaptation.[32] It did not matter whether a monastery was located on Mount Carmel or across the seas, in a solitary place or in a city, provided it was essentially a true Carmel, regardless of the circumstances. But it could only be such if the *Rule's* essential elements were preserved untarnished – the *eremitical, community* and *apostolic* dimensions – with whatever priority or emphasis the religious chose to give them. They all flowed from the hidden spring of the word, pondered and assimilated in praying hearts, and were all three inseparably linked in the Carmelite charism.

Pondering with Mary[33]

So far, we have made no reference to Mary. Her silence in the gospels is reflected in the silence of the *Rule*. She is the Spirit-filled woman of prayer silently 'pondering' the word which she 'treasured' in her heart (Lk 2:19.51). Her prayer is the heartbeat of every praying Carmelite, 'pondering the Lord's law day and night' (#10). The term 'pondering' comes to us from the first psalm (Ps 1:2; cf. Jos 1:8). It is deeply laden with the rich implications of the bible's wisdom and apocalyptic traditions, associated with obscure mysteries awaiting further clarification. It connotes puzzling over something that still needs understanding.[34] Mary kept the enigmatic words of the angel in her heart, awaiting their final unfolding through the light of the Spirit in God's time. But the prayer of 'pondering' involves not only grasping the meaning of obscure sayings. It also requires us to live by them, putting them into practice. It calls for openness to God and to the strangeness of his ways. Mary is attentive to God's time for the full revelation of the mystery entrusted to her, pondering it continually without ever fully grasping it. As the first disciple of her Son,[35] she is called to constant surrender to God's word – wonder, surprise, bewilderment, anxiety, concern, pain. Clothed in Mary's scapular,[36] Carmelites put on her mind, heart and prayer. We ponder the richness of the *Rule* with her, always searching for its relevance here and now, open to new ways of living it and understanding its hidden, mysterious meanings in the light of the Spirit.

Moving with the Spirit

The greeting at the beginning of the *Rule*, 'blessing of the Holy Spirit' (#1), would seem to be designed precisely for that purpose: to dispose recipients for openness to the Spirit. And we read in the final paragraph of the *Rule*: 'our Lord, at his second coming, will reward anyone who does more than he is obliged to do' (#24). Albert now withdraws from the scene. He has captured the charism in legal terms, as far as it is possible. For the rest, a vast silence, like the silence of the gospels, descends and opens up space for the Spirit. The written word is not a 'sacred and untouchable' text exhausting all the possibilities of Carmelite living, nor is it a dead letter.[37] So much of the charism can never be adequately expressed in rules and regulations. But quickened by the Spirit, the *Rule* becomes a many-faceted text, always open to deeper understanding like the gospels, and admitting new forms of Carmelite life in response to the 'signs of the times'.

Looking at the *Rule* in this light, we think of the gospel teaching: '[The Spirit] will remind you of all I have said to you' (Jn 14:26). This 'recalling' is not just to remind Carmelites of the letter of the law. The Spirit will point out the relevance of the text here and now as time unfolds. The silence, once the *Rule* has ended, bears the same message as the gospels: 'I have yet many things to say to you but you cannot bear them now' (Jn 16:12). The words of the *Rule* await the further light of the Spirit. 'He will make known to you the things that are to come' (Jn 16:13), we are told in the gospels. The perspective widens into an unknown future of growth, expansion and development. It is the same Spirit who will lead us into all truth (Jn 16:13) – the full richness of a charism that can never be adequately expressed in words. That charism is embodied in a definitive *Rule* but our grasp of it is always partial.

Besides, the Spirit works in a 'spiral' movement,[38] advancing new possibilities for anyone who, as the *Rule* says, 'does more than he is obliged to do' (#24), inviting us constantly to reassess our calling in changing times, but taking us back again and again to the criterion of the *Rule*: the admonishment, with its final words, to use 'common sense [which] is the guide of the virtues' (#24). There is great originality and freedom in the way the *Rule* is slanted by Albert and later by Innocent IV. But for a balanced interpretation of everything 'over and above', we must return repeatedly to the essential elements: the *eremitical,* the *community* and the *apostolic* aspects.

Good works, good works is the acid test for Teresa (IC VII:4:6) – action in the gospel sense of whoever 'hears the word of God and does it' (cf. Lk 8:21). Of such listening was born the recent venture of the Joint Carmelite Forum meetings in Ireland and Great Britain, with participation by all branches of the family accepting and respecting the differences of emphasis that distinguish one group from another.[39] Each lifestyle is the fruit of a profound and prayerful listening to the *Rule* in the light of the Spirit. 'Look to the future, where the Spirit is sending you,' wrote John Paul II in *Vita Consecrata*, 'in order to do even greater things' (#110). This is the 'more', the 'over and above', of which the *Rule* speaks. The Church is filled with the wonders of the Spirit, who 'breathes where it wills' (Jn 3:8). We must be ready at all times to expect the unexpected from God.

Notes

1   An earlier version of this chapter was delivered as a talk at the Joint Conference on the Carmelite *Rule* at Dalgan Park, County Meath on August 27th, 2002.

2   *Dei Verbum* (*Dogmatic Constitution on Divine Revelation*) 19.

3   'The sacred authors wrote the four Gospels, *selecting* some things from the many which had been handed on by word of mouth or in writing, reducing some of them to a *synthesis, explicating* some things in view of the situation of their churches...' (*ibid.* 19; italics mine).

4   For a scholarly exposition of this approach to the gospels, containing the English text of the *Instruction Concerning the Historical Truth of the Gospels* (1964), see Augustin Bea, SJ, *The Study of the Synoptic Gospels: New Approaches and Outlooks* (English version edited by Joseph A. Fitzmyer, SJ), London & Dublin: Geoffrey Chapman, 1965; also Brown, *Reading the Gospels with the Church, op. cit.,* pp. 9-20 & 87-90.

5   The implications are further explained in ch. 1, note 6.

6   As an aid to entering and recreating Palestine in the time of Jesus, see Jerome Murphy-O'Connor, OP, *The Holy Land: An Oxford Archaeological Guide from Earliest Times to 1700*, Oxford & New York: Oxford University Press, 1998.

7   To understand the culture and milieu into which Jesus was born, see Seán Freyne, *The World of the New Testament* (New Testament Message 2), Wilmington, Delaware: Michael Glazier, 1980.

8   I wish to acknowledge my debt to such pioneering studies as: Michael Mulhall, OCarm (ed.), *Albert's Way: The First North American Congress on the Carmelite Rule*, Rome: Institutum Carmelitanum / Barrington, Illinois: The Province of the Most Pure

Heart of Mary, 1989; *The Rule of Carmel: New Horizons*, Rome: Editrice 'il Calamo', 2000; and the masterly study, Kees Waaijman, *The Mystical Space of Carmel: A Commentary on the Carmelite Rule*, Leuven: Peeters (The Fiery Arrow Collection), 1999.

9   For an exploration of Carmelite spirituality in relation to the sacred places of the Holy Land, see *A Biblical Prayer Journey in the Holy Land, op. cit.*

10   For the origins of the Order, see Joachim Smet, OCarm, *The Carmelites: A History of the Brothers of Our Lady of Mount Carmel*, vol. I: *Ca. 1200 A.D. until the Council of Trent*, Barrington, Ill: Carmelite Province, 1975; Peter-Thomas Rohrbach, OCD, *Journey to Carith: The Sources and Story of the Discalced Carmelites*, Washington, DC: ICS Publications, reprint of 1966 Doubleday edition; Andrew Jotischky, *The Carmelites and Antiquity: Mendicants and their Pasts in the Middle Ages*, Oxford: Oxford University Press, 2002; McGreal, *op. cit.*; Waaijman, *op. cit.*; Elizabeth Ruth Obbard, *Land of Carmel: The Origins and Spirituality of the Carmelite Order*, Leominster: Gracewing, 1999.

11   'Obedience of faith' is an expression characteristic of Paul (Rm 1:5; 16:26), defining faith as obedience. This concept is taken up again by Vatican II: see *Dei Verbum* (*Dogmatic Constitution on Divine Revelation*) 5.

12   See Carlo Cicconetti, OCarm, *La Regola del Carmelo: Origine – Natura – Significato*, Rome: Institutum Carmelitanum, 1973, p. 44.

13   For a woman's perspective on the *Rule*, see Anne Henderson, OCD, 'Rereading the Rule Today: A Woman's Viewpoint', in *The Rule of Carmel: New Horizons, op. cit.*, pp. 143-53.

14   On the biblical implications of the *Rule*, see Camilo Maccise, OCD, 'Biblical Spirituality in the Rule of Carmel', *Carmelite Digest*, vol. 17/1, 2002, pp. 12-32; Giovanni Helewa, OCD, 'The Word of God and the Rule of Carmel', in *The Rule of Carmel: New Horizons, op. cit.*, pp. 21-44; *The Word of God and the Rule of Carmel*, Rome: Casa Generalizia Carmelitani Scalzi (Ongoing Formation, 5), 1996.

15   Augustine, *Quaest. In Hept.*, 2,73 and Jerome, *Commentary on Isaiah*, Prol.

16   Points well made by Dom O. Rousseau, 'The Call to Perfection in Patristic Tradition', in *Vocation*, London: Blackfriars (Religious Life, II), 1952, pp. 8-9.

17   *Dei Verbum* (*Dogmatic Constitution on Divine Revelation*) 25.

18 The following of Christ is the 'fundamental norm' and 'supreme law' of the consecrated life, in that it is the essence of the whole Christian life: see *Perfectae Caritatis* (*Decree on the Appropriate Renewal of the Religious Life*) 2.

19 The Church is a mystery and, as such, is presented in a variety of metaphors to express this *communio*: see *Lumen Gentium* (*Dogmatic Constitution on the Church*) 6-10.

20 #18-19. As a Pauline metaphor for *putting on* Christ and being transformed in him through baptism, see Gal 3:27; Rm 13:14; Col 3:10; Eph 4:24.

21 See Tertullian, *De oratione* 1 and Cyprian, *De dominica oratione* 9 respectively. For an excellent study of the Our Father, with special emphasis on the end-time perspective which fits admirably into the whole thrust of the Carmelite *Rule*, see Raymond E. Brown, SS, 'The Pater Noster as an Eschatological Prayer', *Theological Studies*, 22, 1961, pp. 175-208.

22 See Waaijman, *op. cit.*, pp. 5-6.

23 The original register of Innocent IV in the Vatican Archive (21, f. 465 v) and the oldest manuscripts simply carry the initial 'B'. It was later interpreted as 'Brocard'.

24 This theme of pondering the scriptures in Carmel has been developed in a variety of recent articles: see notes 14 and 28.

25 See ch. 1, section 'Prayer of the heart'.

26 See note 3.

27 See *Lumen Gentium* (*Dogmatic Constitution on the Church*) 6-17.

28 For a modern continuation of the practice of *lectio divina* in community, see the articles of Brigeen Wilson, OCD, *op. cit.*; also, on group *lectio*, see Hugh Clarke, OCarm, *Mary and the Rosary in the light of the Apostolic Letter Rosarium Virginis Mariae of Pope John Paul II, October 16th, 2002*, Faversham: Saint Albert's Press, 2003, pp. 12-3.

29 For the implications of Carmelite life as a collective pilgrimage, see the seminal articles of Emmanuel Nnadozie, OCD: 'The Carmelite Rule in Dialogue with the African Continent', in *The Rule of Carmel: New Horizons, op. cit.*, pp. 59-76 (especially p. 71); 'The Carmelite Rule in Dialogue with Africa: History, Tradition(s) and Gospel Values', *Mount Carmel*, vol. 50/1, 2002, pp. 15-22; 'The Carmelite Rule in Dialogue with Africa: A Way of Transformation', *Mount Carmel*, vol. 50/2, 2002, pp. 34-41.

30 In the eleventh century, Western Europe experienced a renewal of eremitical life and an extensive religious movement with the aim of

following Christ in his poverty. Its adherents called themselves 'The Poor of Christ'. People resolutely renounced the world (*conversio*) in order to dedicate themselves totally to God in a life of penitence (*vivere in sancta poenitentia*). Pilgrimages to the Holy Land were regarded as the highpoint of the penitential life. The hermits of Mount Carmel were part of this movement: see Waaijman, *op. cit.*, pp. 2, 7.

31 See quotation in ch. 2, note 3. For a discussion of the importance of *The Flaming Arrow*, see John Welch, OCarm, *The Carmelite Way: An Ancient Path for Today's Pilgrim*, Leominster: Gracewing, 1996, pp. 27-38.

32 On the need for creative fidelity and adaptation in the light of the 'signs of the times', see Camilo Maccise, OCD, 'The Future of Carmel – A Reflection', *Mount Carmel*, vol. 49/1, 2001, pp. 19-26.

33 For recent works on the Marian tradition of Carmel, see ch. 5, note 1.

34 The implications of these wisdom and apocalyptic traditions, and Mary's attempt to understand the events, are developed in Raymond E. Brown, SS, *The Birth of the Messiah: A Commentary on the Infancy Narratives in Matthew and Luke*, Garden City, New York: Image Books, 1979, pp. 429-31. See also Francis J. Moloney, *Mary: Woman and Mother*, Homebush, NSW: Society of St Paul, 1988, pp. 23-7.

35 See ch. 5, section 'The first disciple'.

36 See ch. 5, section 'Clothed in her mantle'.

37 See Camilo Maccise, OCD & Joseph Chalmers, OCarm, 'Open to God's Future: Circular Letter of the Superiors General O.C.D. and O.Carm., on the occasion of the 750th Anniversary of the Approval of the Rule of Carmel by Innocent IV, 1247 – 1 October – 1997', 1997, in Malley, Maccise & Chalmers, *op. cit.*, pp. 75-98 (see especially pp. 79-80).

38 This 'spiral' movement is typical of the general style of the fourth evangelist, of which the Paraclete passages provide an excellent example. See de La Potterie & Lyonnet, *op. cit.*

39 See the Joint Carmelite Forum issue of *Mount Carmel*, vol. 49/3, 2001; see also the author's 'Carmelite Forum: Sharing a Heritage', *Religious Life Review*, vol. 40, no. 210, 2001, pp. 271-8.

Chapter 4

Rediscovering Saint Joseph: A Gospel Portrait

'Go to Joseph'

Devotion to St Joseph is deeply embedded in the Catholic mind.[1] Always treasured in the 'memory' of the Church, it has, like so many other devotions, had its highs and lows.[2] Joseph is forever closely linked to Jesus and Mary, and so remains always, to some extent, in their shadow. Devotion to him might so easily be jettisoned with our spring-cleaning of flimsy devotions in the wake of Vatican II. And yet, John XXIII in 1961 placed that Council, in anticipation, under the patronage of Joseph 'to whom we have given charge over the Council with complete confidence'.[3]

For Carmelites, dismissal of devotion to Joseph is hardly likely, though the danger is always there. Teresa of Avila constantly interceded with this saint for protection and encouraged others to do the same. She records numerous favours through his intercession, even her own miraculous cure (*Life* 6:8). His feast is 'our titular feast,' she tells us (*Life* 20:5), and she launched her reform in Avila with a new foundation bearing the name of St Joseph's (1562). As she trundled endlessly across Spain, her covered wagon was always shrine to an image of her great patron[4] whom she did not hesitate to call 'founder of this Order'.[5] She has given us a classic text on devotion to him:

I took for my advocate and lord the glorious St. Joseph and earnestly recommended myself to him. I saw clearly that as in this need so in other greater ones concerning honor and loss of soul this father and lord of mine came to my rescue in better ways than I knew how to ask for. I don't recall up to this day ever having petitioned him for anything that he failed to grant. It is an amazing thing the great many favors God has granted me through the mediation of this blessed saint, the dangers I was freed from both of body and soul. For with other saints it seems the Lord has given them grace to be of help in one need, whereas with this glorious saint I have experience that he helps in all our needs and that the Lord wants us to understand that just as He was subject to St. Joseph on earth – for since bearing the title of father, being the Lord's tutor, Joseph could give the Child command – so in heaven God does whatever he commands... And so there are many who in experiencing this truth renew their devotion to him. (*Life* 6:6)

We would all do well to deepen and rekindle our devotion to St Joseph in order that, in the words of John Paul II, 'all may grow in devotion to the Patron of the Universal Church and in love for the Saviour whom he served in such an exemplary manner.'[6]

Heir to the promises

Teresa herself prayed: 'May God deliver us from foolish devotions' (*Life* 13:16). But to honour Joseph is no mere accretion of emotional piety. It is solidly based in the gospels. At first sight, it may not appear so. Not a single word of his has been recorded for us. As Karl Rahner points out, Joseph 'pondered' but 'he spoke little, so little that these words did not have to be transmitted to posterity.'[7] Joseph is not even mentioned in *Mark* and his name appears only rarely in the other gospels.[8] But the few texts that speak of him have profound spiritual implications. They repay careful scrutiny. He is significantly linked through his ancestry with the Old Testament unfolding of God's plan of salvation.

Matthew's genealogy of Jesus begins with Abraham, moves down through David and concludes with 'Joseph the husband of Mary, of whom Jesus was born, who is called Christ' (Mt 1:16). Because of his lineage, the figure of Joseph already invites comparison with Abraham, 'the father of all believers' (Rm 4:11) and the one 'who had received the promises' (Hb 11:17). His family tree also evokes a link with the covenant promised to David. The genealogy stresses the role of David, mentioning him more than anyone else among the ancestors of Joseph, five times in fact (Mt 1:1.6.17). Jesus is to be the *legal* son of 'Joseph, son of David' (Mt 1:20) and so the Davidic promise will be fulfilled: 'I will raise up your son after you... I will make his royal throne firm forever' (2Sam 7:12-13).

This is our first encounter with Joseph in the gospels. He is not a figure peripheral to the story of redemption but already part of the mystery 'kept secret for endless ages' (Rm 16:25; cf. Col 1:26). In him, salvation history approaches a climax. As the husband of Mary, Joseph follows a faith-journey that will lead him, like Abraham (Gn 12:1), into the unknown: 'she will bear a son, and you shall call his name Jesus, for he will save his people from their sins' (Mt 1:21). So, too, as protector of Mary's son, he is the custodian of the heir to the promises and recipient of the Lord's unfailing love promised to David and his descendants: 'I shall not withdraw my faithful love from [you]... I will never take back my love: my truth will never fail' (2Sam 7:15; Ps 88:34). The life of Joseph unfolds as a venture of faith in response to God's love.

'One in mind and heart'

Leo XIII rightly underlines that Joseph, as spouse of Mary, must never be separated from her life and greatness:

> Since marriage is the highest degree of association and friendship, involving by its very nature a communion of goods, it follows that God, by giving Joseph to the Virgin, did not give him to her only as a companion for life, a witness of her virginity and protector of her honour: he also gave Joseph to Mary in order that he *might share*, through the marriage pact, in her own sublime greatness.[9]

As we see in the gospels, Joseph and Mary are inseparably linked. In response to an imperial decree, Joseph went up to Bethlehem 'to be enrolled *with Mary*, his betrothed, who was with child' (Lk 2:5). The shepherds found there '*Mary and Joseph*, and the babe lying in a manger' (Lk 2:16). Yearly, they both went on pilgrimage to the temple: '*his parents* went to Jerusalem every year at the feast of the passover' (Lk 2:41). So Joseph, like Mary and her Son, was steeped in the prayer life and customs of God's people. The book of psalms was his prayer book, too, and the liturgy of Israel's feasts his celebration of God's 'mighty deeds' in the history of his people.

As worried parents, they sought together for the missing Jesus: '*Your father and I* have sought for you anxiously' (Lk 2:48). The evangelist likens them to each other in their failure to understand the words of Jesus: '*they* did not understand the saying which he spoke to them' (Lk 2:50). They were both amazed to find their Son in dialogue with the learned teachers of his day: 'when *they* saw him *they* were astonished' (Lk 2:48).

Later, too, '*his father and his mother* marvelled at what was said about him' by the aged Simeon (Lk 2:33). This final glimpse of Joseph is eloquent of the pain he too must suffer, at one with the pierced heart of Mary. For in his presence, the prophecy was directed to her: 'Behold, this child is set for the fall and rising of many in Israel...and your own soul too a sword shall pierce' (Lk 2:34-35). Joseph must also carry the cross and walk the way of suffering like Mary and every true disciple of her Son.

The hidden life

Joseph is God's chosen instrument called to impart the first lessons to his Son. In Nazareth, Jesus learned from Joseph. There, his first image and idea of the heavenly Father was shaped by Joseph's words and actions: 'One saint alone is destined to represent God the Father,' wrote Jean-Jacques Olier. 'The Father, having chosen this saint to make of him his image on earth, gives him along with himself a likeness of his invisible and hidden nature'.[10] Thérèse of Lisieux said that to know how to pray, she had only to look into the eyes of her own father at prayer (SS, p. 43). Jesus, too, had only to do the same. Perhaps there is an echo of this lesson learned from Joseph when Jesus later taught his disciples the Our Father. He did so only after they had first experienced his own example of communing with his Father while absorbed in prayer: *'when he had ceased praying,* one of his disciples said to him: "Lord, teach us to pray"' (Lk 11:1).

In Nazareth, everything is eloquent with lessons of Joseph's own prayer life 'hidden with Christ in God' (Col 3:3). 'Those souls most sensitive to the impulses of divine love,' wrote John Paul II, 'have rightly seen in Joseph a brilliant example of the interior life.'[11] This quiet saint teaches us in many ways: a lesson in the silence enveloping his moments of deep and intimate communion with God – in a quiet that is filled, as stillness should be, with the presence of Jesus; a challenge to a personal inner life open only to the eyes of God and which he alone rewards in secret (cf. Mt 6:6); an invitation to communion in love with Jesus and Mary – the heartbeat of all true prayer. His life is a witness, also, to the value and dignity of labour done 'in the name of Jesus' – in his service 'working for the Lord and not for men' (Col 3:23); a testimony to the secret value of all activity which derives, as Paul VI explains, 'over and above its economic worth, from the value of those for whose sake it is undertaken';[12] and in his loving service to Mary and Jesus, Joseph has given the example that has made him 'patron of workers', model for all who 'earn their bread by the sweat of their brow' (cf. Gn 3:19).[13]

'Can anything good come out of Nazareth?'

There are some gospel incidents which remind us in passing of how uneventful life really was in Nazareth – a tiny, remote and obscure village where nothing ever seemed to happen and where the rhythm of daily life apparently continued for the most part unnoticed by the world at large. Even one of Jesus' first disciples, Nathanael, remarks on how insignificant and unimportant the village was in the unfolding story of world events: 'From Nazareth? Can anything good come out of that place?' (Jn 1:46).

There is also the reaction of the villagers to the miracles of Jesus during his ministry. This further highlights the obscure origins of Joseph's family. They were 'astounded, saying... "Is not this the carpenter, the son of Mary... and are not his sisters here with us?"' (Mk 6:2-3; cf. Mt 13:54-56). It is all part of the scandal of the incarnation – even for Jesus' own disciples. Some rejected him, saying: 'Surely this is Jesus, the son of Joseph, whose father and mother we know? How can he now say, "I have come down from heaven?"' (Jn 6:42); others accepted him, but only gradually learned to penetrate the veil of mystery surrounding their Master: 'We have found him of whom Moses in the law and also the prophets wrote, Jesus of Nazareth, the son of Joseph' (Jn 1:45).

Joseph, too, wrestled in faith with the mystery unfolding daily before his eyes: the great transcendent God of Israel,

Redeemer of his people, living with him an ordinary, uneventful life unknown to others for some thirty years. Even the family closest to Jesus were scandalised by it: 'When his relations heard of this, they set out to take charge of him; they said, "He is out of his mind"' (Mk 3:21). The experience of Joseph in Nazareth is a lesson for all, anticipating Vatican II's message of the universal call to holiness. The stuff of sanctity is not the extraordinary, the glare of life in the public eye, but the simple, ordinary, humdrum and uneventful chores and duties of daily living and an intimate communing with God who 'walks among the pots 'n' pans' – a holiness within the reach of everyone. Thérèse of Lisieux speaks of Mary and at the same time – unwittingly perhaps – reveals the lesson of Joseph's hidden life: 'It's by *the ordinary way*... / That you like to walk' (PN 54). Paul VI sums up this aspect of Joseph's life beautifully:

> St Joseph is the model of those humble ones that Christianity raises up to great destinies;... he is the proof that in order to be a good and genuine follower of Christ, there is no need of great things – it is enough to have the common, simple and human virtues, but they need to be true and authentic.[14]

A 'just' man

There is one striking feature in Matthew's gospel, announcing Jesus' conception: it is Joseph who holds centre stage and receives the message, not Mary as in Luke's narrative.[15] In Matthew's account, he is mentioned by name four times (Mt 1:18.19.20.24), and the story is told through his eyes. He typifies the 'just', 'upright' or 'righteous' man of the scriptures (Mt 1:19; cf. Ps 1; 111:6-9), like the parents of the Baptist who 'were upright in the sight of God and impeccably carried out all the commandments of the law' (Lk 1:6).

The term 'just' (*dikaios*) has rich biblical implications. It describes the devout Israelite who faithfully observes the law of the Lord. Joseph is obedient to God's commands, at rights with him, *ad-justed* to his will: 'He did as the angel of the Lord commanded him' (Mt 1:24). He 'took Mary as his wife' (Mt 1:20.24), showing himself obedient to God's command like his ancestor Abraham who 'put his faith in God and this was reckoned to him as *righteousness*' (Rm 4:3). God called Joseph and, like the Old Testament patriarch, he obeyed. He is the 'wise' man of Matthew's gospel (cf. Mt 7:24), one of the faithful disciples of Jesus 'who hear the word of God and *do* it' (Lk 8:21; cf. 11:28; Mt 7:24). Not simply a 'listener' to the word, but a '*doer*' of it, one 'who looks into the perfect law, the law of liberty, and perseveres, being no hearer that forgets but a doer that acts' (Jas 1:25). He is that 'wise' follower 'who hears these words of mine,' Jesus says, 'and built his house upon the rock' (Mt 7:24). He stands out in contrast to the 'foolish' man 'who built his house upon the sand' (Mt 7:26) without a solid foundation on the word of God. This makes Joseph the ideal person of prayer in Matthew's gospel.

In the likeness of Jesus' prayer

Each evangelist has his own original portrait of Jesus. For Matthew, he is the obedient Israelite. Nowhere is this more evident than in the example of Jesus at prayer. Rarely does he reveal the content of his communion with his Father. But when he does, we find Jesus heart and soul in total submission to the Father's will.[16]

On one occasion, he raises his voice in praise: 'I give you thanks, Lord of heaven and earth, because you have concealed these things from the learned and the wise and revealed them to little ones... *Such was your gracious will*' (Mt 11:25-26). The context of the prayer is also telling. The evangelist has just presented Jesus as the one rejected by his own people in the towns and cities of his day (Mt 11:20-26). Luke repeats this same prayer of praise word for word (Lk 10:21) and also tells us that Jesus 'rejoiced in the Holy Spirit' at the unfolding of God's design. An invitation follows to confirm for the disciples the lesson of surrender in prayer: 'Learn of me that I am meek and humble of heart' (Mt 11:29) – meek, flexible and in harmony with the truth of his Father's will – just as Joseph was open to the Lord's command.

Again in Gethsemane, the lesson of surrender is the same, but stressed in Matthew's account by comparison with that of Mark and Luke.[17] It is true that in all three gospels, the essence of the prayer lies in submission to God's will: 'Not my will but yours,' Jesus prays (Mt 26:39; Mk 14:36; Lk 22:42). These words are identical in all three descriptions of the prayer. But Matthew heightens the lesson of surrender when Jesus withdraws from his disciples for a second time to pray. Mark leaves the content of his prayer implicit: 'And again he went away and prayed, using the same words' (14:39). In *Matthew*, however, the content is explicit: 'Again, for the second time, he went away and prayed, "My Father... *your will be done*"' (26:42). These words are identical with the third petition of the Our Father found only in Matthew (6:10). The 'just' man prays after the example of Jesus: in obedience to the Father's will – like Joseph who, as we shall see presently, is the ideal disciple of *Matthew*.

Pondering the law of the Lord

But first we recall a description of the 'just' man in the first psalm as one 'who ponders [the Lord's] law day and night' (1:2; cf. Jos 1:8). These same words we find again at the heart of the Carmelite *Rule* to describe the calling to a life of prayer (#10). There is no mistaking the striking parallel. Moreover, the climax of the psalm concludes with a significant contrast: 'the Lord guards the way of the *just* but the way of the wicked leads to doom' (Ps 1:6). This psalm forms an insightful meditation, preliminary to a prayerful reading of Matthew's gospel. Both have the same appeal and challenge. This voice from Israel's past blesses the one who follows the way of the just and 'whose delight is the law of the Lord' (Ps 1:2). By contrast with the wicked, he is one who does not 'linger in the way of sinners nor sit in the company of scorners' (Ps 1:1). We see Joseph, the 'just' man, 'considering' the demands of God's law to dismiss an apparently unfaithful wife. Then, with compassion and sensitivity, 'unwilling to put her to shame, he resolved to send her away quietly' (Mt 1:19).[18] We can only surmise the inner turmoil of his questioning, resolved at last through God's word: 'do not be afraid to take Mary as your wife' (Mt 1:20). But now he is plunged still deeper into a mystery of faith that will take an eternity to unfold: 'what is conceived in her is of the Holy Spirit' (Mt 1:20).

Like the 'just' man of the psalm, Joseph's 'ponderings' are the perennial spring of his actions. Acceptance of God's word will also yield for him the lasting fruit of a tree that strikes its roots deep into 'the flowing waters' of a life-giving stream: 'and all that he does shall prosper' (Ps 1:3). Like Mary, who 'ponders' and 'treasures' the word in her heart (Lk 2:19.51), Joseph, too, 'considers' and acts in the light of God's law, reflects on it and turns it over in his mind (*enthumêthéntos*: Mt 1:20). This makes him a faithful disciple, a true contemplative, and an untarnished reflection of the praying Jesus in Matthew's gospel. No wonder Teresa could write: 'Especially persons of prayer should always be attached to [St Joseph]... Those who cannot find a master to teach them prayer should take this glorious saint for their master, and they will not go astray' (*Life* 6:8). Her words are echoed by John Paul II when he speaks of Joseph's interior life:

The same aura of silence that envelops everything else about Joseph also shrouds his work as a carpenter in the house of Nazareth. It is, however, *a silence that reveals in a special way the inner portrait* of the man. The Gospels speak exclusively of what Joseph 'did'. Still, they allow us to discover in his 'actions' – shrouded in silence as they are – an aura of *deep contemplation*. Joseph was in daily contact with the mystery 'hidden from ages past', and which 'dwelt' under his roof. This explains, for example, why St Teresa of Jesus, the great reformer of the Carmelites, promoted the renewal of veneration to St Joseph in Western Christianity.[19]

The ideal disciple

A parable of Jesus makes this lesson on discipleship clear. It is found only in *Matthew* (21:28-31) and opens up the heart of his gospel. It challenges the listener at the outset: 'What do you think?' Then comes the story. A father told the first of his two sons to go and work in the vineyard. At first he refused, but later 'he repented' and went. He said the same to his second son who agreed, but later refused to go. Then the crucial question: 'Which of the two *did* the will of his father?' The answer is obvious, the first, and with it Matthew opens up the nature of following the call of Jesus: 'Not everyone who says to me, "Lord, Lord" will enter the kingdom of heaven, but the one who *does* the will of my Father in heaven' (Mt 7:21). Discipleship is to *do* God's will – obedience, surrender, bearing fruit in action.

It is this listening in humble submission with readiness to act that also gives prayer its distinctive emphasis in *Matthew*: 'in praying do not heap up empty phrases as the pagans do,' Jesus tells his disciples, 'for they think that they will be heard for their many words' (Mt 6:7). Prayer is not a magic wand that is waved to coerce God into responding to our will. 'Your Father knows what you need before you ask him' (Mt 6:8). Prayer changes *us*, not God; and it gradually brings our wills into harmony with his.[20] Again, Matthew's special form of the Our Father proves the point. His words, 'Thy will be done' (Mt 6:10), are not found in Luke's version of the prayer. This petition is an expansion and deeper understanding by Matthew's community of the first two petitions: God's name is hallowed and his kingdom comes *when his will is done.*[21]

A model of renewal

There is an inner transformation required by submission to God's will. The first son in our parable 'repented' (Mt 21:29) in the gospel sense of that term: a change of mind and heart. New lights, challenges and renewal are essential to deepening prayer. Putting on the mind of Christ required a radical reversal of thinking for those first disciples who, with their new gospel values and beliefs, 'turned the world upside down' (Acts 17:6).

As a man of prayer, Joseph was no exception to this law of inner change. The kingdom had come to him in a new and unexpected way with Jesus and entered his heart with explosive power, making all things new. 'The law was given through Moses; grace and truth came through Jesus Christ' (Jn 1:17). This upheaval was all part of Joseph's faith struggle in surrendering to God's will. The first stage of salvation history fades into the background for him when Jesus' birth is announced: '[Your wife] will bear a son,' he is told, 'and you shall call his name Jesus, for he will save his people from their sins' (Mt 1:21). These words usher in a final stage in God's plan of redemption: 'Abraham rejoiced to think that he would see my day,' Jesus said, 'he saw it and was glad' (Jn 8:56). Joseph too – like every believer – saw it and rejoiced. A new day had dawned.

The old hidden in the new

Matthew's infancy narrative abounds in Old Testament quotations, five in all.[22] Their purpose is clear: to link the early years of Jesus with Israel's past. The evangelist evokes the exodus with the words of Hosea: 'Out of Egypt I have called my son'

(Mt 2:15; Hos 11:1). This gives added depth to his narrative. The story of Israel's liberation from slavery is a central event in her history. It was God's answer to the pleas of his people in bondage: 'I have seen the affliction of my people who are in Egypt and have heard their cries' (Ex 3:7). This captive people living in expectation of redemption are forerunners of the 'little ones' in Matthew's gospel (cf. Mt 11:25) – the 'poor of Yahweh', like Zechariah and Elizabeth, Simeon and Anna in Luke's gospel, yearning for the Messiah to set them free, just as Joseph and Mary longed with total trust in God's promises. 'Deliver us, O Lord, from our bondage as streams in dry land' (Ps 125:4).

The Joseph of *Matthew* is a man to whom God spoke in dreams (1:20; 2:13.19.22) and who went down to Egypt to save the child with his mother: 'Rise, take the child and his mother, and flee to Egypt' (2:13). This portrayal of Joseph is clearly designed, in broad outline, to recall the Joseph of the Old Testament.[23] He, too, was a man to whom God communicated through dreams (Gn 37:5-10; cf. 37:19) and who saved his people by going down to Egypt (Gn 45:5; 50:20). This story of salvation is continued in the liberation of God's people from the slavery of Egypt by the hand of Moses. The name 'Jesus' itself fits into this striking parallel between Matthew's story of Joseph and the story of his predecessor, prototype and namesake. As the angel announces to Joseph: 'you will call his name Jesus, for he will save his people from their sins' (Mt 1:21). In fact, the successor of Moses, who continued the saving work of the patriarch Joseph, was called Joshua, meaning 'Jesus'.

This exodus theme is a recurring motif of the gospels. Jesus is led into the desert where he remains for forty days and forty nights – a symbolic re-enactment of Israel's forty years in the desert before entering the promised land. The imagery, symbols and thought-patterns of the wilderness experience occur repeatedly throughout his ministry: the teaching of the Sermon on the Mount parallels the giving of the law on Mount Sinai

(Mt 5-7; Ex 20:1-17); the pillar of fire foreshadows Jesus as 'the light of the world' (Jn 8:12; 9:5; Ex 13:22; 14:24); the water issuing in torrents from the heart of Jesus recalls the water flowing from the rock (Jn 7:38; Ex 17:6); the serpent 'lifted up' in the desert anticipates Jesus 'exalted' on the cross (Jn 3:14-15; Nb 21:8-9); the manna is a symbol of Jesus as 'the bread that has come down from heaven' (Jn 6:41; Ex 16:4); Jesus walks on the waters just as the people passed dry-shod through the Red Sea (Jn 6:19; Ex 14:22). More important still, Moses and Elijah speak with Jesus at the transfiguration about his 'exodus' in Jerusalem (Lk 9:31), the new exodus of his passion-resurrection.[24] Moreover, Jesus himself describes his return to the Father as his hour 'to pass out of this world to the Father' (Jn 13:1) – a reference, on the eve of the passover, to Israel's celebration of the exodus.

It is highly significant that Matthew again makes Joseph the main figure when he evokes the flight to Egypt, thereby linking him inseparably with Jesus and Mary in a renewal of Israel's desert experience. As Teresa writes: 'I don't know how one can think about the Queen of Angels and about when she went through so much with the Infant Jesus without giving thanks to St Joseph for the good assistance he then provided them both with' (*Life* 6:8). We must also remember that Matthew wrote his gospel with hindsight, and his infancy stories provide an explanation in anticipation of the final outcome of the gospel story. Joseph's sharing with Mary and her Son takes on deeper significance in the full light of the paschal mystery.

A desert experience
The gospel provides us with several details and intimations to fill out the general picture of Joseph's exodus experience. The *Hosea* reference already quoted – 'Out of Egypt I have called my son' (Hos 11:1) – is a good example. The prophet's words are recorded in *Matthew* (2:15) for readers already familiar with the

text in its rich and meaningful original context. The quotation is closely linked to these words in the same verse of *Hosea*: 'When Israel was a child, *I loved him*'. This recalls the Yahweh of the Sinai covenant: 'a God merciful and gracious, slow to anger, and abounding in steadfast love and faithfulness' (Ex 34:6). This abiding love is a recurring theme when the psalmist recounts the wilderness experience: 'He brought Israel out from their midst, for his great love is without end; arm outstretched, with power in his hand, for his great love is without end… Through the desert his people he led, for his great love is without end' (Ps 135:11-12.16). Joseph walks into the unknown in response to a God who 'first loved us' (1Jn 4:19). His venture of faith in the wilderness is the story of a love.

The psalmist also records the trials of the people on the march: 'He remembered us in our distress, for his great love is without end. And he snatched us away from our foes, for his great love is without end' (Ps 135:23-24). Salvation history repeats itself in the life of Joseph. The story of Herod's 'furious rage' (Mt 2:16) and his resolve 'to search for the child to destroy him' (Mt 2:13), together with his subsequent slaughter of the innocents (Mt 2:16), are there to prove it. The Lord warned Joseph to 'flee to Egypt' (Mt 2:13) in order to escape the wiles and machinations of a tyrant bent on thwarting the designs of God. The forces of evil were also arrayed against God's people when he led them through the desert: 'Pharaoh and his force… Nations in their greatness… Kings in their splendour' (Ps 135:15.17.18). These same powers of darkness were unleashed against Joseph. But for all the many hardships he had to endure, he always had one firm anchor for his faith: 'his great love is without end'.

A testing of faith

Joseph's faith was to be sorely tested. We can fill in some of the details from Luke's story of the finding in the temple (Lk 2:41-

51). This brief episode is a kind of play within a play. It anticipates in miniature the dramatic movement of Luke's whole gospel, which also begins and ends in the Jerusalem temple (1:9; 24:52-53). Each year, the parents of Jesus went up to Jerusalem, we are told, to celebrate the passover (Lk 2:41). Luke's gospel also unfolds for the most part within an extended journey of Jesus to Jerusalem – to his 'departure' there, the new exodus of his passion-resurrection. The journey of Joseph to Jerusalem with his family is an anticipation, in miniature, of this final journey of Jesus and at a deeper level should be interpreted in the light of the passion and death.

Joseph is not the main figure in Luke's temple scene but he is linked there significantly with Mary's testing of faith. '*They* did not understand the saying which he spoke to them,' we are told, in words reminiscent of their reaction to Simeon's prophecy: '*His father and his mother* marvelled at what was said about him' (2:33). What a testing of faith also for his parents in their anguish and pain, when they failed to find Jesus among their relatives 'and went back looking for him everywhere' (2:45). There is the same concern again for both of them in Mary's words: 'Your father and I have sought for you anxiously' (2:48). This was their experience of abandonment – quite literally – by God, like the spiritual testing of Israel in the desert, anticipating the cry of Jesus on the cross: 'My God, my God, why have you forsaken me?' (Mk 15:34). Nor was this Joseph's only troubled moment and testing of faith.

We can only surmise something of Joseph's earlier trial, before the angel reassured him about Mary: 'what is conceived in her is of the Holy Spirit' (Mt 1:20). The Pharisees would later chide Jesus with words that echo Joseph's acute problem by challenging the very legitimacy of Mary's child: '*We* were not born in fornication' (Jn 8:41). The implication is, of course, that Jesus was. All through his life Joseph had to grapple in faith with this possible misunderstanding of Mary's 'seemingly scandalous pregnancy',[25] an enigmatic situation beyond human comprehension.

The faith of God's people was also tested in the desert. It failed. Even the faith of their leader wavered. So it was Joshua, not Moses, who would lead a new generation into the promised land (Dt 32:52; Jos 1:2). The people 'murmured' and so 'I took an oath in my anger,' God said, '"Never shall they enter my rest"' (Ps 94:11). No word of protest, however, is recorded on the lips of Joseph. His trust never faltered: 'Take the child and his mother' (Mt 2:13). He did so immediately, and 'left *that night* for Egypt' (Mt 2:14) – a spontaneous and generous response to God's word. Never a murmur, then, to this echo of God's command to Abraham: 'Go from your country and your kindred and your father's house to the land that I will show you' (Gn 12:1). Joseph was also called to make the patriarch's final sacrifice repeatedly in spirit, as he treasured the words of Simeon and pondered them in his heart: 'This child is set for the fall and rising of many in Israel, and for a sign of contradiction' (Lk 2:34). Already Joseph shared, in anticipation with Mary, in the paschal mystery – through this first intimation of her Son's rejection – continually dying and rising spiritually with him. It was all part of Joseph's call to walk in faith the pilgrim path of God's people in the wilderness: 'I will lead the blind in a way that they know not, in paths that they have not known I will guide them' (Is 42:16).

The silences of the gospels

Such, then, is the evidence of the scriptures about the life of Joseph. He fades quietly into the background after the finding in the temple when Jesus is only twelve, and leaves the limelight to Mary and her Son as the story of salvation history continues to unfold. A paraphrase of Thérèse's words about Mary provide us with a fitting postscript to our gospel portrait of this great silent man of prayer: I must see his real life, not his imagined life. I'm sure that his real life was very simple. Spiritual writers should present him to us as imitable, bringing out his virtues, saying that he lived by faith just like ourselves, giving proofs of this from the gospel (cf. LC, p. 161).

But we can also probe the silences of the scriptures about him in the light of the Spirit at work in the praying Church. The liturgy confirms the rich fruits of our exploration and provides new vistas for us to understand better the mystery of Joseph's life. The importance of the link with Abraham and David is confirmed. Joseph marks the closing of the Old Testament, we are told: 'In him the dignity of the prophets and patriarchs achieves its promised fulfilment.'[26] He is described as 'Nearest of all men to the heart of Jesus'[27] – truly a beloved disciple entrusted with God's most precious treasures, Mary and her Son. The mass preface of his feasts reminds us once again that he is the 'just man', a 'wise and loyal servant, whom you [Father] placed at the head of your family', and that 'With a husband's love he cherished Mary, the virgin Mother of God.' So, too, 'With fatherly care he watched over Jesus Christ your Son'. All this and much besides confirms Bernardine of Siena's general rule: 'Whenever divine grace selects someone to receive a particular grace, or some especially favoured position, all the gifts for his state are given to that person, and enrich him abundantly.' Then he adds: 'This is especially true of that holy man Joseph.'[28] These words speak volumes to every lover of this saint and open up endless possibilities for exploring more deeply in prayer the lessons of this humble carpenter from Nazareth.

The liturgy also leaves us with a final picture of Joseph denied us in the gospels. He is summoned at the end 'into the joy of [the] Lord'.[29] An example to all of us of a life well lived, he is truly the one of whom the psalmist sings: 'Happy the man who fears the Lord, who takes *delight* in his commands... He is a light in the darkness for the *upright*: he is generous, merciful and *just*' (Ps 111:1.4). But he is also our companion on our final exodus out of this world 'into the joy of the Lord'. He is 'Saint of the dying,' the liturgy tells us, 'blest with Mary's presence', resting 'in death...in the arms of Jesus'; and so, the Church prays: 'at our ending, Jesus, Mary, Joseph, / Come to assist us!'[30] He is not just guardian of the Redeemer, patron of the universal Church and model for all workers. He is also our brother who walks the pilgrim way of faith with us and will still be there as the evening's shadows lengthen, forever linked inseparably with Mary and her Son, to welcome us home into the fullness of eternal life.

Notes

1   Since the proclamation by Pius IX, on December 8th, 1870, of St Joseph as patron of the universal Church, every pope (except John Paul I) has advanced the theology of and devotion to this saint. Documents of special note are: *Quemadmodum Deus* (the proclamation of 1870) and *Inclytum Patriarcham* (1871) by Pius IX, *Quamquam Pluries* (1889) by Leo XIII, *Bonum Sane* (1920) by Benedict XV, *Divini Redemptoris* (1937) by Pius XI, *Novis Hisce Temporibus* (1962) by John XXIII and *Redemptoris Custos* (1989) by John Paul II. For a study of Joseph and his place in salvation history, see the encyclopaedic work of Francis L. Filas, SJ, *Joseph: The Man Closest to Christ*, Boston: St Paul, 1962; also the recent collection of articles from various perspectives: Michael D. Griffin, OCD (ed.), *Saint Joseph in the Third Millennium: Traditional Themes and Contemporary Issues*, Hubertus, WI: Teresian Charism Press, 2000.

2   The growth of devotion to St Joseph is charted from the first centuries of the Church right up to Vatican II in Andrew Doze, *Discovering Saint Joseph*, Slough: St Paul Publications, 1991, pp. 13-91.

3   Quoted in Griffin (ed.), *op. cit.*, p. 153.

4   See Tomas Alvarez (dir.), *Diccionario de Santa Teresa: Doctrina e Historia*, Burgos: Editorial Monte Carmelo, 2002, pp. 387-8.

5   *Ibid.*, p. 388. See, too: *St Joseph: Father and Founder of the Teresian Carmel*, Rome: Casa Generalizia Carmelitani Scalzi (Ongoing Formation, 7), 1998. Jerónimo Gracián, friend and collaborator of Teresa, entitled bk. V, ch. 4 of his *Summary of the Excellencies of St Joseph* (1597): 'St Joseph as the Holy Patron of St Teresa of Avila'.

6 *Redemptoris Custos* (*Guardian of the Redeemer*) 1.

7 From Karl Rahner, SJ, 'A Homily for the Feast of St. Joseph', in Griffin (ed.), *op. cit.*, p. 335.

8 Mt 1:16.18.19.20.24; 2:13.19; Lk 1:27; 2:4.16; 3:23; 4:22; Jn 1:45; 6:42 (also Lk 2:43 in the *King James Version*).

9 *Quamquam Pluries* (*On Devotion to St Joseph*) 3, quoted in *Redemptoris Custos* (*Guardian of the Redeemer*) 20.

10 From his work, *La Journée chrétienne*, quoted in Doze, *op. cit.*, p. 67. The image of Joseph as a reflection of the Father should not be identified with some portrayals of him in popular art as an old man with flowering staff which derives mostly from the apocryphal writings: see especially *Protoevangelium of James* 9:1-2.

11 *Redemptoris Custos* (*Guardian of the Redeemer*) 27.

12 Address on January 5th, 1964, in *Divine Office*, vol. I, p. 207.

13 Joseph was proclaimed patron of workers by Benedict XV in 1920; the commemoration of St Joseph the Worker on May 1st was established by Pius XII in 1955. A list of the most important recent papal documents presenting Joseph as the 'model' of workers is given in *Redemptoris Custos* (*Guardian of the Redeemer*), note 35.

14 *Discourse*, March 19th, 1969 and *Insegnamenti* 7, 1969, as quoted in *Redemptoris Custos* (*Guardian of the Redeemer*) 24.

15 See the helpful discussion by Raymond E. Brown, SS, 'The Annunciation to Joseph (Matthew 1:18-25)', in Griffin (ed.), *op. cit.*, pp. 66-79.

16 For the theme of prayer in *Matthew*, see the author's *Prayer – The Heart of the Gospels, op. cit.*, pp. 25-52.

17 David M. Stanley provides an excellent comparative study of the different gospel accounts of the Gethsemane scene: see his *Jesus in Gethsemane*, New York: Paulist Press, 1980.

18 This is the 'private, domestic, "no fault" manner before two witnesses (or perhaps with none at all) not out of suspicion, but in order to cooperate with God's plan', as expressed by Larry M. Toschi, OSJ, in Griffin (ed.), *op. cit.*, p. 14. See also below: section 'A testing of faith' and especially note 25.

19 *Redemptoris Custos* (*Guardian of the Redeemer*) 25.

20 See ch. 2, section 'Not changing *God*, changing *us*'.

21 The significance of this point is developed at length in the author's *Prayer – The Heart of the Gospels, op. cit.*, pp. 47-8.

22 Mt 1:23 (Is 7:14); Mt 2:6 (Mic 5:2); Mt 2:15 (Hos 11:1); Mt 2:18 (Jer 31:15); Mt 2:23 ('prophets': a citation perhaps of Judg 13:5; 16:17).

23 See the comprehensive list of parallels between the two Josephs by Larry M. Toschi, OSJ, in Griffin (ed.), *op. cit.*, pp. 25-8. This comparison, which some might take to be pious reflection, was made official, as it were, when stated by Pius IX at the opening of his decree, *Quemadmodum Deus*.

24 See ch. 2, section 'The word of the cross'.

25 See Brown, 'The Annunciation to Joseph', *op. cit.*, p. 68 and his discussion, in this same article, of the problem for Joseph of Mary's miraculous pregnancy: section 'The Dilemma of a Just Man', pp. 69-73. For an alternative interpretation – in which Joseph is in awe at the sacred pregnancy, doubting not Mary's apparent unfaithfulness, but dubious about how he should act under the circumstances – see Ignace de La Potterie, SJ, *Mary in the Mystery of the Covenant*, New York: Alba House, 1992, pp. 37-65. See also note 18.

26 Bernardine of Siena, Sermon 2, on St Joseph, in *Divine Office*, vol. II, p. 60*.

27 From feast of St Joseph, March 19th, hymn at Morning Prayer, in *Divine Office*, vol. II, p. 61*.

28 Bernardine of Siena, *op. cit.*, pp. 59-60*.

29 *Ibid.*, p. 60*; cf. Mt 25:21.23.

30 From feast of St Joseph, March 19th, hymn at Morning Prayer, in *Divine Office*, vol. II, p. 61*.

Chapter 5

Mary – Woman of Prayer: A Gospel Exploration

The mystical memory of Carmel

Right from the beginning, Mary is inseparably linked with prayer in the Carmelite tradition.[1] The conflict with the false prophets of Baal ended, we find Elijah, the father of all Carmelites, at prayer: he 'climbed to the top of Carmel and bowed down to the earth, putting his face between his knees' (1Kgs 18:42). Then his servant called out: 'Behold, a little cloud like a man's hand is rising out of the sea' (1Kgs 18:44), a harbinger of the rain about to fall in torrents. In the mystical memory of Carmel, this 'cloud' is seen as a symbol of the mother of Jesus. It is, of course, technically a legend. But it is not some kind of insubstantial myth. Titus Brandsma, a Carmelite priest who died at Dachau, draws attention to the symbolic import of this cloud for Carmelites. He refers to passages in the Old Testament, such as that of the cloud that overshadowed the ark of the covenant in the wilderness, and shows that a cloud was often the sign of God's presence among his people.[2] So, to see the cloud rising from the sea as a symbol of Mary's place in the mystery of the incarnation is fully in harmony with the Old Testament as a foreshadowing of the New. In the words of Paul, 'the reality is Christ' (Col 2:17). From the outset, the mother of Jesus as a woman of silent prayer has always been a vital inspiration, essential and integral to the Carmelite charism.

Discovering the mystery of Mary

The contemplative lifestyle of the first hermits on Mount Carmel is well attested. They are significantly defined, in what is called the *Rubrica Prima* of the Order, as those 'who are true lovers of the solitude of this mountain for the sake of *contemplating heavenly things*'.[3] A little chapel, now in ruins and once dedicated to our Lady, still bears witness today to Mary's presence in the first Carmelite community. These men of prayer, who became known as the 'Brothers of St Mary of Mount Carmel', were in turn to shape their own special devotion to the mother of God gradually with the passage of time. She was honoured among them as *Domina*, that is, 'Lady' or 'Mistress'; as 'Mother', 'Mother of Carmel'; also as 'Sister' in the faith, sometimes called simply 'Carmelite' – in other words, 'one of us'.[4] As intimacy with Jesus grew in prayer, so too did intimacy with his mother. The two are inseparable.

There is a beautiful parallel between the discovery of Mary in the Carmelite tradition and in the tradition of the early Church. The first believers also discovered the mystery of Mary gradually in prayer. As they penetrated the message of her Son under the Spirit's action, new perspectives on her place in the plan of redemption began to emerge. We too may discover Mary again, in a new way perhaps, if we explore how the mystery of her presence in the early Church gradually unfolds in the light of the scriptures.[5]

In Paul: 'born of a woman'

The letters of Paul are the earliest New Testament witness to the faith of the Church. Curiously, Mary is never referred to in them, with not even a passing mention of her name. We find, however, a reference to God's Son as 'born of a woman, born under the law' (Gal 4:4). But 'born of a woman' merely tells us that Jesus shared our common human lot, like John the Baptist: 'among those born of women, no one is greater than [he]' (Mt 11:11). Paul's letters never reflect on the mother of God. This is not to say that Paul himself did not ponder the mystery of Mary: his writings are not a complete expression of his mind. Reading Paul is like eavesdropping, as it were, on a telephone conversation – listening to one side of a dialogue, usually about a specific problem. We would not have a single word from Paul about the eucharist, for example, were it not for excesses in the Christian community at Corinth (1Cor 11:20-34). But it is significant that the heart of the gospel message could be expressed by Paul without referring to Mary. However, the four gospels mention her, and there is one reference besides in *Acts* (1:14). These passages may be brief, but they are revealing.

In Mark: 'who are my mother and my brothers?'

It is indeed sobering to find that Mary appears only once during the public ministry in the first three gospels. If we look at *Mark*, generally regarded as the first of the gospels, we read:

> And his mother and his brothers came; and standing *outside* they sent to him and called him. And a crowd was *sitting about him*; and they said to him, 'Your mother and your brothers are *outside*, asking for you.' And he replied, 'Who are my mother and my brothers?' And looking around on those who *sat about him*, he said, 'Here are my mother and my brothers! Whoever does the will of God is my brother, and sister, and mother.' (Mk 3:31-35)

The setting for this scene is significant. The family of Jesus ('mother' and 'brothers') are outside, Jesus is inside; and looking around at 'those who sat about him,' he says, 'Here are my mother and my brothers!' The distinction between the two groups, one outside and the other inside, is clearly marked. We know that one becomes a member of the family of the chosen people by birth from a Jewish mother. But with Jesus we now have a radical change. There is no indication in *Mark* that Jesus is including his mother and brothers among the members of his new family who do the will of God. Mark does not exclude them, but he distinguishes sharply between his family relatives by natural birth and the family of his disciples.

Mary is also mentioned a second time in *Mark* (6:1-6). The people of Nazareth take offence at the local carpenter-boy turned teacher:

> Where did this man get all this? What is the wisdom given to him? What mighty works are wrought by his hands! Is not this the carpenter, the son of Mary and brother of James and Joses and Judas and Simon, and are not his sisters here with us? (6:2-3)

Jesus replies that a prophet is 'not without honour, except in his own country, *among his own relatives* and in his own house' (6:4). Such an attitude to the family of Jesus is part of the radical starkness of Mark's gospel. There Jesus is alone and misunderstood, even by his own relatives who 'set out to seize him', saying, 'He is beside himself' (3:21). Clearly, we find little in *Mark* to suggest the Church's later developed understanding of Mary's deep relationship with her Son.

In Matthew: 'is not this the carpenter's son?'

The situation is different in *Matthew* and *Luke*. Both evangelists wrote their gospels to affirm, at least partly, the Church's deeper understanding of Mary. They knew something about Jesus of which Mark seems to be ignorant: namely, that Jesus was conceived virginally of Mary by the Holy Spirit. This is their special contribution to the Christian memory. It is a new insight which begins to transform the early community's grasp of the mystery of Mary. In *Matthew* we find a moderate development of this understanding; in *Luke* the development is dramatic.

In Matthew's infancy story (chs. 1-2), Joseph is the main figure. Mary herself is only mentioned: as mother of the child by the Holy Spirit. But this insight already transforms the Marcan scene of his mother and brothers who come asking for Jesus (Mt 12:46-50; cf. Mk 3:31-35). Matthew has parallels to all the Marian references in *Mark*, but no mention of 'his relatives' who say, 'He is beside himself.' A mother who conceived Jesus by the Holy Spirit is inevitably much more sensitive to the identity of her Son. So, when Jesus returns to Nazareth and the village people ask where he got this 'wisdom', Matthew is more reverential than Mark: Jesus is not called a 'carpenter', but 'the carpenter's son' (Mt 13:55; cf. Mk 6:3). Moreover, Matthew states simply: 'A prophet is not without honour except in his own country and in his own house' (Mt 13:57); he omits Mark's addition, 'among his own relatives' (Mk 6:4). It is unthinkable that a mother who conceived miraculously of the Spirit would not honour her Son. Already the mystery of Mary is deepening in the prayerful understanding of the church.

In Luke: 'let it be done to me according to your word'

We find an even more profound development in the Church's understanding of Mary in *Luke*. His infancy narrative (chs. 1-2) centres entirely on Mary. As in *Matthew*, she is the woman who conceives of the Holy Spirit (Lk 1:35). But she is now a living character who speaks rather than merely being mentioned. We hear her responding to God's will in her own words: 'Let it be done to me according to your word' (1:38). So, she is the first in the gospels to hear the word of God and do it; and she continues as such throughout the ministry of Jesus. This accords her a unique place as a disciple of her Son (Lk 8:19-21; 11:28).

The scene of the mother and brothers who come asking for Jesus is also changed, even more radically, in *Luke* (8:19-21). As with *Matthew*, gone is Mark's reference in the context of 'his relatives' who say, 'He is beside himself' (Mk 3:21). But unlike both *Matthew* and *Mark*, there is no sharp contrast in *Luke* between the family of believers and the natural family (cf. Mk 3:31-35; Mt 12:46-50). Jesus' mother and brothers stand 'outside' wishing to see Jesus, but in *Luke* Jesus does not ask, 'Who are my mother and my brothers?', nor does he point by way of contrast to those inside as his mother and brothers. Rather, he affirms without distinction, 'My mother and my brothers are those who hear the word of God and do it' (Lk 8:21). Significantly, Luke places the scene after the parable of the sower and the seed (8:4-15). The seed that falls on good soil and bears fruit a hundredfold relates to those who, like his mother, 'hear the word of God and hold it fast' (8:15; cf. 8:21).

We will find Mary again still listening faithfully to the word of God, when we catch our final glimpse of her in Luke's writings, as she waits at Pentecost for the coming of the Spirit at the heart of the praying Church (Acts 1:14). The early church's understanding of Mary deepens enormously in *Luke*. But there are more revealing insights yet to come.

In John: 'woman, behold your son'

John has no infancy narrative. The natural birth of Jesus is not his main concern. However, Mary appears twice in his gospel (2:1-11; 19:25-27). At Cana, she stakes a family claim to her Son and asks for help: 'They have no wine' (2:3). Mary had already expressed a family claim in the temple: 'Son, why have you done this to us? Your father and I have sought for you anxiously' (Lk 2:48). Jesus replies that he 'must be about [his] Father's business' (Lk 2:49). The Father's will takes priority. The lesson of Cana is the same: 'What is that to you and to me? My hour has not yet come' (Jn 2:4).[6] Initially, Jesus distances himself from his mother's request, but Mary gives priority to the will of her Son: 'Do whatever he tells you' (2:5). Only then does Jesus manifest his glory at her request. She is a woman of faith who obeys her Son – she is his true disciple.[7]

So far, John's understanding of Mary is in line with the more developed insights of Matthew and Luke as the woman who listens to the will of God and does it. But the presence of Jesus' mother on Calvary constitutes a radical advance on the common tradition of the other gospels (Jn 19:25-27). At the foot of the cross stand the mother of Jesus and the beloved disciple. Their personal names are not given. They are historical, but they are also representative figures. The nameless disciple serves as a model for all those whom Jesus loves. The mother of Jesus, too, has a figurative role. She is not simply the physical mother of Jesus. Like Mark (3:21), John deals harshly with the physical relatives called the 'brothers' of Jesus, who did not believe in him (Jn 7:5). Mary is the mother of the beloved disciple – that is, the mother of every disciple. On the cross we have a definitive answer to the question, 'Who are my mother and my brothers?' Jesus points to the two beside him: 'Woman, behold your son… Behold your mother' (Jn 19:26-27). They are his true family: a mother and a brother in the new family of believers.

Prayer is the key
The church has already come a long way in its understanding of Mary. In *Mark*, the natural family bond between Jesus and his mother stands out in striking contrast to the spiritual bond uniting the new family of believers. This deeper spiritual family bond between Mary and her Son gradually emerges in *Matthew*. In *Luke*, she is the first to follow her Son and is the *model* of every disciple 'who hears the word of God and does it'. In *John*, finally, she is the *mother* of every true disciple.

Clearly, the mystery of the mother of Jesus forms part of the Church's inner, secret treasure. It unfolds gradually through deepening prayer, as it did for the early Church and as it did later in Carmel. In both traditions, Mary and her Son are inseparable: we cannot isolate the one from the other. Discovering the mystery of Mary is the fruit of ripening faith, and prayer is the key that unlocks the mystery.

'Let it be done to me'
It is true the gospels have little to tell us – explicitly – about Mary's prayer. But when we first meet her, we already find her alone communing with God and open to receive the Spirit. The annunciation to Mary is a prayer scene. The Lord is with her, and the loving exchange between them reflects Teresa's description of prayer as 'an intimate sharing' (*Life* 8:5). God takes the initiative and comes in love to meet Mary, not because she first loved him but because he first loved her who is the 'most highly favoured one' (Lk 1:28) – the object of his special love. She is perplexed at the promise to give her a son, and responds in turn with a love that dares to question 'how'. She struggles for a deeper understanding. Light dawns gradually: 'The Holy Spirit will come upon you' (Lk 1:35). Elizabeth of the Trinity invokes the Holy Spirit in words which clearly show how imbued she was with the spirit of Mary's prayer: 'O consuming Fire, Spirit of Love, "*come upon me*", and create in my soul a kind of incarnation of the Word: that I may be another humanity for Him in which He can renew His whole Mystery' (PT; italics mine).[8]

A 'sign' brings further light to Mary: her cousin once 'sterile' is already fruitful by the power of God. For Mary, the mystery remains, but the impossible is possible: 'with God all things are possible' (Lk 1:37). And so in faith she accepts his word: 'Let it be done to me' (1:38). Here we find a basic pattern to her prayer. It is a questioning in faith, with a challenge to surrender to God's word under the action of the Spirit. For John of the Cross, this is why Mary is not just a woman of prayer but *the* woman of prayer: 'for she was always moved by the Holy Spirit' (3A 2:10) – like every true follower of her Son in Paul's understanding of discipleship: 'All who are led by the Spirit of God are sons of God' (Rm 8:14).

A Spirit-filled woman

Mary is a perfect embodiment of that prayer which is intimately linked by Luke with the gift of the Spirit. We could almost call it his own original insight. It is true that we find the same prayer of Jesus in *Matthew* and *Luke*: 'I give you thanks, Father, Lord of heaven and earth...' (Mt 11:25; Lk 10:21). But Luke gives it his own slant. He, not Matthew, introduces the prayer by saying: 'He rejoiced *in the Holy Spirit* and said...' So, Jesus himself prays under the powerful impulse of the Spirit. In the baptism scene, too, it is only Luke who tells us that Jesus was '*praying*' when the Holy Spirit descended upon him (Lk 3:21-22). He is launched on his public ministry by the Spirit received in deep communion with his Father. Even the words of the Our Father in *Luke*, 'Your kingdom come' (11:2), are given a curious but significant interpretation by some Fathers of the Church. They read it as: 'May your Holy Spirit come'.[9] They caught the meaning. That is precisely what we pray for: the coming of God in his kingly power through the gift of the Spirit. Elsewhere, Luke repeats word for word the teaching of Matthew on prayer: 'ask...seek...knock' (Lk 11:9; cf. Mt 7:7). However, it is Luke, not Matthew, who says, 'How much more will your heavenly Father give the *Holy Spirit* to those who ask him!' (Lk 11:13; cf. Mt 7:11).

The gift of the Spirit is God's response to Mary's prayer – to every prayer. As the woman whose heart is filled with the Spirit, she is model for a distinguished line of Carmelite saints. When Teresa wanted to describe the effects of prayer, she borrowed a phrase from the psalms: 'Dilatasti cor meum' (IC IV:1:5; 2:5). It means literally: 'you have expanded my heart' (Ps 118:32).

John of the Cross seems to be echoing this idea in the final line of perhaps his greatest poem, 'The Living Flame': 'how tenderly you swell my heart with love.' So, too, Thérèse of Lisieux is in line with the Mystical Doctor in her description of prayer as 'something…which expands my soul,' she says, 'and unites me to Jesus' (SS, p. 242). More recently, Mother Teresa of Calcutta repeated the same lesson: 'Prayer enlarges the heart until it is capable of containing God's gift of himself. Ask and seek, and your heart will grow big enough to receive him and keep him as your own.'[10] Prayer is always answered: God gives the Spirit as he did to Mary, in response to her prayer. It is God's gift of himself – the infallible response to every prayer.

A woman who believes

Impelled by the Spirit, Mary sets out to share her new experience with her cousin Elizabeth. Their meeting is also a prayer, a giving-and-receiving in the Spirit. It is like a family liturgy. Together they celebrate the wonders of salvation: 'Elizabeth was filled with the Holy Spirit and she exclaimed with a loud cry, "Blessed are you among women, and blessed is the fruit of your womb!"' (Lk 1:41-42). Mary's *magnificat* of praise in response translates her experience of the Spirit's action into a witness of hope for the hungry, the thirsty, the lowly and the poor who have nothing – the *anawim*, the 'little ones' like Mary who trust entirely in God's mercy: 'he puts down the mighty from their thrones and raises the lowly; he fills the hungry with good things' (Lk 1:52-53). Her cousin Elizabeth also voices her praise of Mary's faith: 'Blessed is she who has believed...' (Lk 1:45). In this lies the key to Mary's prayer – a faith, like Abraham's, that believes the word of God in the face of the seemingly impossible. To quote John Paul II: 'In the expression "Blessed is she who believed", we can therefore rightly find *a kind of "key"* which unlocks for us the innermost reality of Mary'.[11] But belief is never static, and the faith of Mary leads her on a long journey of faith, seeking an ever deeper understanding of her Son.

A pilgrim of faith

'The power of the Most High will *overshadow* you' (Lk 1:35). Again, Elizabeth of the Trinity identifies with Mary in her prayer, invoking God with this same word rich in Old Testament implications: 'You, O Father, bend lovingly over Your poor little creature; "*overshadow* her", seeing in her only the "Beloved in whom You are well pleased"' (PT; italics mine).[12] Luke's expression connects Mary's journey in faith with the exodus of God's people and points to her as the new ark of the covenant which God *overshadows* with his presence (Ex 40:34-35). Mary is directly linked in this way with Israel's journey through the wilderness. Just as God descended and was present in the ark, he now comes upon Mary and *overshadows* her as the new tabernacle, or temple, of his presence among his pilgrim people. In her, salvation history repeats itself.

Like the children of Israel, Mary lives a painful desert testing of faith. She experiences the absence of God: 'Your father and I have sought for you anxiously' (Lk 2:48). She walks in darkness and does not always understand: 'They did not understand the saying which he spoke to them' (Lk 2:50). She knows the cost of inner change in a growing relationship with her Son: 'Did you not know that I must be about my Father's business?' (Lk 2:49). At Cana, she feels the distance that separates them both: 'What is that to you and to me?' (Jn 2:4).[13] But her pain gives way to concern for others: 'They have no wine' (Jn 2:3). Her final spoken prayer in the gospels is once again an act of faith in surrender to her Son: 'Do whatever he tells you' (Jn 2:5).

This faith of Mary gives meaning to her years of quiet obscurity in the gospels while she 'ponders' (Lk 1:29; 2:19.51) and in her heart 'listens to the word of God' (cf. Lk 8:21; 11:28). Thérèse of Lisieux describes for us the witness value of

Mary's uneventful, hidden life of faith in Nazareth with these words: 'Mother, full of grace, I know that in Nazareth / You live in poverty, wanting nothing more. / *No rapture, miracle, or ecstasy / Embellish your life...*' (PN 54). She further explains in the same poem why Jesus wanted his mother to 'be plunged into the night, in anguish of heart'. It is because he 'wants you to be the example / Of the soul searching for Him in the night of faith.' It is all part of Mary's faith-journey in openness to the action of the Spirit – her prayer experience.

A spiritual mother

Mary's path leads her to Calvary where the sword of Simeon's prophecy will finally pierce her soul (Lk 2:35). Like Abraham,[14] she stands poised for the sacrifice, which Luke surely had in mind when he described Mary's offering of Jesus in the temple: 'Take your son, your only son whom you love, and offer him on a mountain that I will show you' (cf. Gn 22:2). Her child is 'a sign of contradiction' (Lk 2:34), a Suffering Servant 'despised and rejected... a worm and no man' (Is 53:3; Ps 21:7). She had been told: 'He will be great...' (Lk 1:32). Her questioning then is voiceless now: 'How can this come about?' (Lk 1:34). The unspoken answer is the same: 'With God all things are possible' (Lk 1:37). Again, her faith is tested. Wordless, she stands at the cross – powerless beside her powerless Son. Her silence is the language of love. This is her prayer: to be there, one-with-him in weakness, a presence. But all her pains are pangs in a new birth: 'When a woman is in labour, she has pain, because her hour has come' (Jn 16:21). Mary's anguished prayer bears fruit. She is the final gift of her crucified Son to his beloved disciple, and in him she becomes spiritual mother to us all: 'Behold your mother' (Jn 19:27).

It would be easy to be sceptical about the mystery of Mary as mother of all believers – taking it as little more than a fabrication of simple piety. But it is a truth, and one that is deeply embedded in the gospels. Jesus gave Mary to us in a real sense as our spiritual mother on Calvary. That is the deeper meaning of his words. Technically, they constitute a 'revelatory formula' made up of three elements: '*said... saw... Behold*'. This same word pattern is found elsewhere in *John*: 'Jesus *saw* Nathanael coming towards him and *said*, "*Behold* an Israelite in whom there is no guile"' (Jn 1:47); and John the Baptist introduces Jesus to his disciples with the same word sequence: 'He *saw* Jesus coming towards him and *said*, "*Behold* the Lamb of God"' (Jn 1:29.35). The formula reveals the deeper spiritual import of a person's role in God's mysterious plan of salvation. As 'an Israelite in whom there is no guile', Nathanael, meaning 'gift of God', is a man without deceit and a type of every true disciple who comes to Jesus and is given to him by the Father (Jn 6:37). So, too, Jesus is 'the Lamb of God' in a deep spiritual sense. His death as a sacrificial victim on the cross is described in terms identifying him as the new passover lamb: 'Not a bone of his shall be broken' (Jn 19:36; cf. Ex 12:46; Nb 9:12; Ps 33:21). 'Jesus said to his mother, "Woman, behold your son"' (Jn 19:26) and with his words discloses to faith the mystery of her role in the plan of salvation and constitutes her universal mother of the Church. Then Jesus said to John, 'the disciple whom he loved' and the type of every believer, 'Behold your mother' (Jn 19:27). And with these words he opens up, in the person of John, the deeper relationship of every follower of Jesus to Mary as spiritual mother.

Carmelite resonances

This scene of Jesus with Mary and the beloved disciple at the foot of the cross takes on special significance in the Carmelite prayer tradition. The gospel description ends with the evangelist's final comment: 'And from that hour the disciple took her into his own home' (Jn 19:27) – literally took her to 'his own', that is, made her his own. John of the Cross echoes this in verse:

The Virgin comes walking,
the Word in her womb:
could you not give her
place in your room?[15]

This is not simply a question couched in spatial terms, referring
to an actual room. It is a reminder that Mary has taken us into
the room of her *heart* and invites us to return the favour:
opening the room of our hearts to her, and making an inner
space there to receive her. But perhaps no Carmelite has
expressed the whole mystery of Mary from the perspective of
Calvary, with all its deeper and wider implications, better than
Edith Stein in her inspired prayer, '*Juxta crucem tecum stare*':

Today I stood with you beneath the cross
And felt more keenly than I ever did before
That you, beneath the cross, became our mother.

Even an earthly mother's faithful love
Desires to carry out her son's last wish.
Yet, you are the handmaid of the Lord,
And surrendered in your entire being and life
To the Being and Life of God made man.
You have taken us into your heart,
And with the lifeblood of your bitter pains
Have purchased life that's new for every soul.

You know us all: our weakness and our wounds.
You also know the spark of heaven's flame:
Your Son's love longs to take it
And pour it on us – an eternal blaze.
You guide our steps with care,
No price for you too high
To lead us to the goal.

But those whom you have chosen as companions here,
Surrounding you one day at the eternal throne,
We now must stand, with you, beneath the cross
And purchase, with our lifeblood's bitter pains,
This spark of heaven for those priceless souls
Whom God's own Son bequeaths to us, His heirs.[16]

Mary at the heart of the Church

Our final glimpse of Mary finds her in the midst of the disciples, 'constant in prayer' (Acts 1:14). The parallel with our first glimpse of her at prayer is striking. Then she opened to receive the Spirit, now she opens to receive him yet again. Then she listened faithfully to the word promising her a Son, now she listens faithfully to the word promising an extension of her Son, as it were, in a Spirit-filled Church. Then she was a witness in the Spirit to the 'mighty deeds' of God at work in her, now she is one with witnesses preparing to proclaim these 'mighty deeds' anew in the Spirit. A unique and silent witness at the heart of a praying Church, she is our mother and the first disciple of her Son; a sister, too, who stands beside us and who once walked, like us, in faith – on a pilgrim's journey of prayer.

The first disciple

That is how John Paul II speaks of Mary: as 'the first disciple'.[17] This marks a renewed approach to the mystery of Mary in relation to her Son: '*in a sense* Mary as Mother became *the first "disciple" of her Son*,' writes John Paul II, 'the first to whom he seemed to say: "Follow me"'.[18] She is not on a pedestal; she is part of the human race; she is one-of-us, one-with-us – a disciple, a believer. For many, this is a new slant on Mary but it is perfectly in line with the Carmelite tradition of Mary as our sister in the faith, and it is as old as the gospels: 'A woman in the crowd raised her voice and said to him, "Blessed is the womb that bore you, and the breasts that you sucked!" But Jesus replied, "Blessed rather are those who hear the word of God and keep it!"' (Lk 11:27-28). Here, Jesus is only taking up again what he said earlier in the gospel: 'My mother and my brothers are those who hear the word of God and do it' (Lk 8:21). Yes, it is a great thing to be mother of our Saviour in the flesh, but there is something about her even greater still: to be a disciple, a believer. 'Indeed…she did the Father's will,' Augustine says, 'and it is a greater thing for her that she was Christ's disciple than that she was his mother.'[19] It was, as he shows, a greater thing for her to believe in Jesus than to carry him in her womb. Mary is someone we can imitate. Paul VI explains how. His words are worth recalling in full:

> First, the Virgin Mary has always been proposed to the faithful by the Church as an example to be imitated not precisely in the type of life she led, and much less for the socio-cultural background in which she lived and which today scarcely exists anywhere. She is held up as an example to the faithful rather for the way in which, in her own particular life, she fully and responsibly accepted the will of God (cf. Lk 1:38), because she heard the word of God and acted on it and because charity and a spirit of service were the driving force of her actions. She is worthy of imitation because she was *the first and the most perfect of Christ's disciples.* All of this has a permanent and universal exemplary value.[20]

Clothed in her mantle[21]

For Carmelites, the brown scapular of Our Lady of Mount Carmel is a constant reminder that Mary is our mother and to be imitated as the first disciple of her Son. It binds us to her as one who cares for her children and lovingly protects them at all times, especially at the hour of death. It also links us to her as a model for every disciple called to walk, like her, in the footsteps of her Son. There is no short cut along the gospel path. The scapular is not an amulet or charm. This sign of Carmel implies a twofold relationship of love between mother and child. It is both gift and obligation, with a seven-centuries-old spiritual meaning approved by the Church from which it derives its value and significance. As a symbol, it does not depend on the exact historical truth of an apparition to Simon Stock, once erroneously linked with it, but stands for a personal decision to follow Jesus as Mary did. It introduces those who wear it to the family of Carmel, calling them to 'quiet time' with the Lord in prayer and contemplation. But it is not designed solely for Carmelites. It is 'a treasure for the whole Church,' John Paul II tells us, 'a "habit", that is a permanent way of Christian living, made up of prayer and the interior life… a sign of "covenant" and of reciprocal communion between Mary and the faithful. It expresses in a concrete way the gift, which Jesus, while hanging on the cross, made of his Mother to John, and through him to us. It also gives expression to Jesus' commitment of the beloved disciple and of us to Her, who thus became our spiritual Mother.'[22]

'Our tainted nature's solitary boast'

Mary's privileges do not remove her from the lot of redeemed humanity. 'We know very well that the Blessed Virgin is Queen of heaven and earth,' Thérèse of Lisieux assures us, 'but she is more Mother than Queen; and we should not say, on account of her prerogatives, that she surpasses all the saints in glory just as the sun at its rising makes the stars disappear from sight. My God! How strange that would be! A mother who makes her children's glory vanish! I myself think just the contrary' (LC, p. 161). Mary's privileges, apart from her unique dignity as the mother of God, are firmly anchored in the destiny of *every* faithful disciple of her Son. At Lourdes, Mary said, 'I am the Immaculate Conception.' Some of the finest minds of the early centuries of the Church struggled long, and often in vain, to explain how such a privilege could ever be possible. But Mary was conceived without sin through God's application to her beforehand of the grace of her Son. Every human person needs that grace. This is a basic privilege of every disciple. We believe that Mary was the first one to whom it was accorded, and it was done at the moment of her conception. It invests her with a unique dignity; it is an enormous grace, a staggering mystery. But it does not remove her from the level of graced *humanity*. She still remains one of us, one-with-us. She was the first of the disciples and receives in anticipation the basic privilege to which every follower of Jesus is heir.

'Mary, the Immaculate and ever-virgin Mother of God, when the course of her earthly life was over, was taken up, body and soul, into heaven.'[23] With these words, Pius XII declared that the doctrine of our Lady's assumption into heaven is an essential truth of faith. At the time, it provoked an outcry and protests in response – another formidable obstacle, it was claimed, in the path of ecumenism! The Church had managed perfectly well without this dogma for nineteen hundred years, so why proclaim it now? But the prophets of doom cannot appeal to the verdict of history to justify their concern. Mary has experienced the resurrection of the body promised by her Son. Every Christian is destined to be raised bodily from the dead. We believe that this happened to Mary in anticipation of the final judgment. Once again, she was the first to enjoy a privilege promised to every believer because she was the first disciple of her Son. These privileges of Mary are in line with the Church's understanding of the gospel message on discipleship. The proclamation of the assumption is a call to the world – to our world – not to abuse the body, by either despising it or adoring it, for it is destined to share with Mary in the glory of her Son's resurrection. 'Today the virgin Mother of God was taken up into heaven to be the beginning and the pattern of the

Church in its perfection,' the mass preface for the feast of the assumption tells us, 'and a sign of hope and comfort for your people on their pilgrim way.'

Our first glimpse of Mary in the Carmelite tradition was inseparably linked with Elijah at prayer and with the vision of 'a little cloud like a man's hand…rising out of the sea' beneath the slopes of Carmel. The Church leaves us with a final glimpse of her at the end of her earthly life, assumed into heaven like Elijah, where she continues, like the same prophet in the Jewish tradition, to intercede for the people of God.[24] There she lives, still linked in prayer with the seer of Carmel, as she stands like him before the face of God to intercede unceasingly for her children, 'now and at the hour of our death'.

Notes

1   Note recent works on the Marian tradition of Carmel: Donald W. Buggert, OCarm, Louis P. Rogge, OCarm & Michael J. Wastag, OCarm (eds), *Mother, Behold Your Son: Essays in Honor of Eamon R. Carroll, O.Carm.*, Washington, DC: The Carmelite Institute, 2001; John F. Welch, OCarm (ed.), *Carmel and Mary: Theology and History of a Devotion*, Washington, DC: The Carmelite Institute, 2002; Joseph Chalmers, OCarm, *Mary, The Contemplative*, Rome: Edizioni Carmelitane, 2001; Emanuele Boaga, OCarm, *The Lady of the Place: Mary in the History and in the Life of Carmel*, Rome: Edizioni Carmelitane (Carmelitana Series, 2), 2001.

2   From his lecture, *In the Spirit and Strength of Elias*, given at the Catholic University in Washington, summer 1935: see Titus Brandsma, *The Beauty of Carmel*, Dublin: Clonmore & Reynolds / London: Burns, Oates & Washbourne, 1955, p. 32.

3   See the Latin text in Adrianus Staring, OCarm, *Medieval Carmelite Heritage: Early Reflections on the Nature of the Order*, Rome: Institutum Carmelitanum, 1989, p. 40; italics mine.

4   For a discussion of the titles by which Mary has been known in the Order, see Boaga, *op. cit.*

5   I am deeply indebted to an excellent article by Raymond E. Brown, SS: 'Mary in the New Testament and in Catholic Life', *America*,

May 15th, 1982, pp. 374-9. See, too, the author's 'Discovering Mary with the Gospels', *Mount Carmel,* vol. 48/1, 2000, pp. 43-8; also: *A Biblical Prayer Journey in the Holy Land, op. cit.,* pp. 501-37.

6   Albert Vanhoye, SJ interprets these words as questions: 'What is that to you and to me? My hour, has it not yet come?' and develops John's subtle use of questions, open to a 'yes' or 'no' answer, for a deeper understanding of the text: see his *'Interrogation johannique et exégèse de Cana* (Jn 2,4)', *Biblica,* vol. 55, 1974, pp. 157-67.

7   See note 17.

8   See also ch. 1, note 16 for reference to an alternative translation. Elizabeth wrote this well known prayer at the end of a retreat on 'The Mystery of the Incarnation' as she reflected on the annunciation.

9   Gregory of Nyssa and Maximus Confessor: see Joachim Jeremias, *The Prayers of Jesus,* London: SCM Press, 1967, p. 83.

10   Malcolm Muggeridge, *Something Beautiful for God: Mother Teresa of Calcutta,* London: Collins, 1971, p. 66.

11   *Redemptoris Mater* (*Mother of the Redeemer*) 19; see this same document (#14) for parallels between the faith of Mary and of Abraham.

12   The official translation, 'cover her with Your shadow', has been rendered here as 'overshadow her'. See also note 8.

13   See note 6.

14   See note 11.

15   Marjorie Flower, OCD (tr.), *Centred on Love: The Poems of Saint John of the Cross,* Varroville, NSW: The Carmelite Nuns, 1983, p. 46.

16   Based on the translation in *Mount Carmel,* vol. 50/1, 2002, p. 64.

17   Mary is the first disciple of her Son. See John Paul II, *Redemptoris Mater* (*Mother of the Redeemer*) 20; Paul VI, *Marialis Cultus* (*Devotion to the Blessed Virgin Mary*) 35.37; Raymond E. Brown, SS, 'Mary in the New Testament and in Catholic Life', *op. cit.,* p. 379.

18   *Redemptoris Mater* (*Mother of the Redeemer*) 20.

19   From Sermon 25, in *Divine Office,* vol. III, p. 409*.

20   *Marialis Cultus* (*Devotion to the Blessed Virgin Mary*) 35; italics mine.

21   See Camilo Maccise, OCD, 'The Brown Scapular of Our Lady of Mount Carmel', *Mount Carmel,* vol. 48/1, 2000, pp. 59-61; Hugh Clarke, OCarm, *Mary and the Brown Scapular,* The Carmelite

Charitable Trust, 2002; Joseph Chalmers, OCarm & Camilo Maccise, OCD, 'With Mary the Mother of Jesus (*Acts* 1,14): Letter of the Superiors General O.Carm and O.C.D. on the occasion of the 750th Anniversary of the Carmelite Scapular', May 16th, 2001, in Malley, Maccise & Chalmers, *op. cit.*, pp. 159-78 (see especially pp. 167-74).

22 John Paul II, 'Letter on the occasion of the Carmelite Marian Year to the OCarm and OCD Generals', March 25th, 2001, #4-5. See also the general superiors' document inspired by that letter: Chalmers & Maccise, 'With Mary the Mother of Jesus (*Acts* 1,14)', *op. cit.*

23 *Munificentissimus Deus* (*The Assumption of the Blessed Virgin*) 44.

24 'Elijah intercedes in heaven on behalf of Israel': Marie-Joseph Stiassny, NDS, '*Le Prophète Élie dans le Judaïsme*', in Bruno de Jésus-Marie (ed.), *op. cit.*, vol. II, p. 214.

Epilogue

We have seen how the word of God permeates the Carmelite charism. Such is also the case with the Carmelite saints. Each one of them is a unique embodiment of the spirit of Carmel, living and expressing it in their own original way. But for all their differences of time and culture, age and temperament, they convey a common teaching on prayer that is deeply embedded in the scriptures, especially in the gospels.

For Teresa of Avila, the great reformer of Carmel, silent prayer is 'nothing else than an intimate sharing between friends', and she explains: 'it means taking time frequently to be alone with Him who we know loves us.' Her description evokes immediately the words of Jesus: 'I have called you friends because I have made known to you everything I have heard from my Father' (Jn 15:15). This is the essence of authentic Carmelite prayer: an intimacy with God in a close communion of love – a sharing that requires extended time, solitude and perseverance, if the relationship is to grow and deepen. Here, the great doctor of prayer links her teaching with the core of the gospel message on love. She values prayer essentially as an expression of that love in the depths of the human heart.

John of the Cross, her great spiritual mentor, 'father of my soul' as she called him, and her companion in the work of reform, repeats her teaching with his own original slant. For him, contemplation is 'nothing else than a secret and peaceful and loving inflow of God, which, if not hampered, fires the soul in the spirit of love'. His words are a beautiful expression, and original interpretation, of the gospel teaching on the infallible response to every prayer: 'How much more will the heavenly Father give the Holy Spirit to those who ask him!' (Lk 11:13) – the Spirit who himself is that same 'inflow of God', enkindling within us the fire of love in the darkness of faith. The 'flame', the Mystical Doctor explains, is the Holy Spirit.

Thérèse of Lisieux, the most recent Carmelite Doctor of the Church, has herself been called 'a word of God'. It is the gospel that was canonised today, commented one priest in St Peter's Square, when the 'greatest saint of modern times' had just been raised to the altar. Her definition of prayer, too, is rich with gospel resonances: 'For me, *prayer* is an aspiration of the heart, it is a simple glance directed to heaven, it is a cry of gratitude and love in the midst of trial as well as joy; finally, it is something great, supernatural, which expands my soul and unites me to Jesus.' Such prayer itself unites her to Jesus who 'raised his eyes to heaven' (Jn 17:1), communing with his Father in a cry of gratitude and love: in times of joy – 'He rejoiced in the Holy Spirit and said, "I thank you, Father"' (Lk 10:21), and in times of trial – 'Save me from this hour' (Jn 12:27). Prayer expands the soul of Thérèse. For Teresa of Avila, this is an effect of authentic Carmelite prayer, one which she describes borrowing the words of the psalm, 'you have expanded my heart' (Ps 118:32), and which John of the Cross echoes in the concluding line of perhaps his finest poem, 'The Living Flame of Love': 'how tenderly you swell my heart with love.'

The message of Elizabeth of the Trinity, a close contemporary of Thérèse, also draws its inspiration from the gospels. With her unerring theological depth, she writes: 'We possess our Heaven within us, since He who satisfies the hunger of the glorified in the light of vision gives Himself to us in faith and mystery, it is the Same One! It seems to me that I have found my Heaven on earth, since Heaven is God, and God is [in] my soul. The day I understood that, everything became clear to me. I would like to whisper this secret to those I love so they too might always cling to God through everything, and so this prayer of Christ might be fulfilled: "Father, may they be made perfectly one!"' Heaven is indeed where God is, and God – Father, Son and Holy Spirit – is in the heart of every believer. Jesus tells us: 'we will come to them and make our home in them' (Jn 14:23) – one of Elizabeth's favourite gospel phrases. This profound mystery of the indwelling of the Trinity is central to Elizabeth's teaching on prayer, just as it is the foundation on which Teresa of Avila builds the inner journey of prayer towards the centre of the soul, where God sits enthroned in the human heart. In all her writings, Elizabeth does indeed still 'whisper' this secret for all to experience in their silent communing with God, so that the longing of Jesus himself, in his priestly prayer, may be fulfilled: 'that they may become perfectly one' (Jn 17:23).

One of the more recent Carmelite saints is Edith Stein, martyred in Auschwitz. She echoes the gospel lesson on silent listening to the word of God as the source of all fruitful activity in the Church: 'We need hours for listening silently and allowing the Word of God to act on us until it moves us to bear fruit in an offering of praise and an offering of action.' The image readily comes to mind of Martha's sister Mary, who 'has chosen the better part', sitting at the feet of Jesus and listening to his word; so, too, does the reminder of Jesus himself that 'blessed are those who hear the word of God and *do* it' (Lk 11:28). As a Jew steeped in the Old Testament, Edith confidently draws a telling image of prayer from *Genesis*: 'Prayer is a Jacob's ladder on which the human spirit ascends to God and God's grace descends to people.' Edith Stein is a bridge between the Old Testament and the New, and this may well be her most original contribution to the mystery of Christian prayer. But perhaps nowhere does she capture better the spirit of Teresian prayer – the 'intimate sharing between friends' – than with her words which are also reminiscent of Jesus' teaching his disciples to pray in their 'inner room' (Mt 6:6): 'The only essential is that one finds, first of all, a quiet corner in which one can communicate with God as though there were nothing else, and that must be done daily.' All Edith's greatness as writer and lecturer, philosopher and feminist, is peripheral to the depth of her inner life of silent listening to the word in prayer. As she herself assures us: 'Prayer is the highest achievement of which the human spirit is capable.'